Shine

"I love the idea that our calling as Christ followers is where our deep gladness and the world's deep hunger intersect (as Francis Schaeffer said), so when I found out my dear friend Allison was writing a book on essentially that very subject, my heart did backflips! *Shine* is a literary match that will ignite the fuel in your soul purposed to burn brightly for the sake of the gospel."

Lisa Harper, bestselling author and Bible teacher

"Allison Allen and I are quite opposite to the casual observer. I'm a man, she's a woman. I'm short, she's tall. I'm bald, she's a brunette. She can dance, I cannot. She can sing, I cannot. I skate, she doesn't. But we both love Jesus and have stepped on some pretty big stages to perform under immense pressure. In this book Allison shares stories of conquering fear, pain, and rejection that uniquely paved the way toward growth, joy, and wisdom. You will most definitely be inspired."

Scott Hamilton, Olympic figure skating champion;
sports commentator; inspirational speaker; cancer survivor

"I loved Allison the moment I laid eyes on her. She is kind and warm, funny and deep. Through her beautifully transparent story, you and I are encouraged to step out of the shadows of fear and self-doubt and in Jesus's name, shine!"

Sheila Walsh, author of *In the Middle of the Mess*;
co-host of *LIFE Today*

"Is your heart 'a chapel full of dreams'? Take Allison's hand—she knows the narrow path to true brilliance. I've been warmed by her presence and inspired by her gifts. Trust me, Allison is a candelabra of hope for those who long to shine."

Patsy Clairmont, speaker; artist; author of *You Are More Than You Know*

"Imagine the director of your favorite Broadway production inviting you to take a tour behind the curtain—to see all the trade secrets from the glowing tape on the floor to the lighting fixtures above. And imagine that while you're there, the Lord shows up to speak directly to the place in your soul that's been desperate for a word from him. That is the encouraging journey to which Allison Allen invites her readers."

Teasi Cannon, author of *My Big Bottom Blessing: How Hating My Body Led to Loving My Life*

"*Shine* is so inspiring, honest, and thought-provoking. I am confident it will cause whoever reads it to take a step of bravery into what it is that God has planned for them."

Jeremy and Adie Camp, songwriters and recording artists

"Allison points us to the Light of the World as *the* place to find our spot to stand on this stage of life and show up in the full measure of ourselves—not as a selfish pursuit of ego fulfillment but as an offering to the Lord of the Dance, the ultimate Casting Director."

Anita Renfroe, comedian and author

"I love the way Allison weaves her written words into the vibrant visual images of her life. In beautiful and practical ways, she makes it possible for every woman to identify with so much of what she says. Readers will be drawn in new and compelling ways to keep Christ at the center of their hearts and lives."

Cynthia Ulrich Tobias, author of *A Woman of Strength and Purpose*

"If you think books on 'being real' and 'finding your authentic self' have fallen prey to cliché, read Allison Allen's *Shine*! Allison's hunger to live free from her self-made typecast made me want to settle for nothing less. You—and I—can step off the treadmill of performing for who knows who, in order to land the role of a lifetime, the role you alone were created to fulfill."

Michele Pillar, speaker; Grammy-nominated singer; author of *Untangled*

"In *Shine*, Allison Allen lends a seasoned voice to the postmodern conversation about value. With heart and hope, she implores us to emerge from the shadows of fear-based social constructs and take our place in the light of the One who transcends them all."

Constance Rhodes, founder and CEO of FINDING*balance*, Inc.; author of *The Art of Being: Reflections on the Beauty and the Risk of Embracing Who We Are*

"In her beautifully written and scripturally sound book, Allison Allen has constructed a wildly creative manifesto for women who long to move from the spiritual shadows into the glorious light of Jesus's calling. *Shine* is a book with your name on it."

Steve Berger, senior pastor, Grace Chapel, Leiper's Fork, TN; speaker; author of *Between Heaven and Earth: Finding Hope, Courage, and Passion through a Fresh Vision of Heaven*

Shine

STEPPING INTO THE
ROLE YOU WERE
MADE FOR

Allison Allen

Revell

a division of Baker Publishing Group
Grand Rapids, Michigan

Published by Revell
a division of Baker Publishing Group
P.O. Box 6287, Grand Rapids, MI 49516-6287
www.revellbooks.com

Printed in the United States of America

Library of Congress Cataloging-in-Publication Data is on file at the Library of Congress, Washington, DC.

ISBN 978-0-8007-2819-9

Some names and details have been changed to protect the privacy of the individuals involved.

The author is represented by Alive Literary Agency, 7680 Goddard Street, Suite 200, Colorado Springs, CO 80920, www.aliveliterary.com.

17 18 19 20 21 22 23   7 6 5 4 3 2 1

For my mother, Patsy

So shines a good deed in a weary world—

Contents

Contents

Dear Friend

I'm edge-of-my-seat excited that you're here. Really, I mean that.

I've been thinking about you for the better part of a year, while asking God to take this wild jumble of stories and stumbles and turn them into something that will speak to the sleeping part of you—that part that longs to wake. Something that builds a stage for your heart to believe that the Maker of All has given you a divine role in his story, as well as a place to shine.

As we begin our journey, I wonder where you are today. I wonder if, like me, you're tired of playing a character and are more than ready to exchange the suffocating pressure to perform for a life of purpose and shining for his glory. Are you feeling an urge to step from the shadows and beeline into the glorious light of the children of God?

Though I use many stories about my life as an actor, I can assure you that this book is not primarily about acting. In his creativity, God has often used the acting life to save me from a life of acting and has shown me how it was on the stage where I first tasted so many kingdom truths I'm coming to savor.

My hope is that these words will become his whispers to you, inviting you by name to drop the brave act. Inviting you to step boldly into your light in Christ. Inviting you to resist a life of hiding and a life lived in "character shoes." Inviting you to believe that no one else's story is as exciting as the one Jesus is penning for you.

And above all, inviting you to shine.

Arise and shine,
Allison

1

All the World's a Stage

For the creation waits in eager expectation for
the children of God to be revealed.

Romans 8:19

I just showed up for my own life.

Sara Groves[1]

I had finally found the perfect place to hide. In the
shadow of a sunburned bush in a nook of a California parking lot, I crouched, hunching into a ball far smaller
than my six-foot-tall self would normally allow. My hand
shielded my face from passersby as tears raced down my
cheeks, dotting my jeans like salty raindrops.

"I don't know. I can't. I just can't," I whispered into the
phone at my ear. "My heart is coming out of my chest. I

don't know. I tried. I can't breathe. I feel like I'm dying. I can't. I can't do it."

The thing I couldn't seem to do—a thing I had done perhaps a thousand times in my life—was act onstage. This particular performance was a one-woman drama about the beauty of anonymously wasting one's life on Jesus. Fifteen hundred of the country's worship leaders and pastors were assembling in the sanctuary as I sat in the parking lot wondering if I needed to call an ambulance because I thought my heart might stop.

This makes no sense, I thought. *Why now?* Why not a million other times along the way? I had made an auspicious stage debut as a bovine in kindergarten and had been at it ever since. From community theater to magnet arts to Governor's School to Carnegie Mellon to Broadway and Women of Faith®, I had relished a life of storytelling on the stage. I had always been able to pull myself together and step onto the stage. Sure, there had been hiccups along the way. No life is without its hiccups. But this? This was different. This was abject fear. Fear of rejection. Fear of failure. Fear of success. Fear of being seen. Fear of feeling fear.

My thoughts were broken by my own ragged breaths. Though I had never experienced a panic attack before, I was pretty sure that was exactly the harrowing beast I was facing in the parking lot. I pulled on sunglasses as I figured out how in the world I would tell the dear friend who had brought me in for the event that I wouldn't be taking the stage. This day, I would be staying in the wings.

I wonder how many of us are hiding in the wings.

Too many of us stand in the shadows, peeking through the side curtains of the stage, watching as monumental God-stories unfold somewhere out there under the lights—stories we ache to join, stories that have the potential to spark faith and kindle hope. Stories that, on our most grace-full days, we suspect we were made for.

But something blocks our way. Something worms down into the stuff we are made of and plants a potent lie. It whispers that it's far better to remain safely shadowed than ever dare to shine. It says that it doesn't really matter if *you* do, because anyone else will do in a pinch. It murmurs that a truly humble Christian woman would demur, hold the curtain open for someone else. It's a lie that says if you do come to the party, please, please, please come as anyone but yourself. *This* is the lie that has left so many of us with spiritual stage fright.

Most of the time the lies enter the scene looking like a pair of unholy twins: fear and shame. I've been stunted and silenced by this terrible duo more times than I care to count. They've been relentless in telling me that not stepping up for the story God has called me to is far safer, far better than to risk entering the stage with Jesus. Safer? I might give the twins that. Risking with Jesus is not necessarily safe; in fact, it can often be downright terrifying. But better? Not on your life. Because nothing is better for us or the people we love than stepping into the great Drama to which God has invited us. Nothing is better than going where he goes. Risking as he risks. Taking the stage when he says, "This is it, kid. See that light pooling out there? Go find it. For this moment and this time, the stage is yours."

15

Every Woman's Stage

You might be thinking, *I've never stood on a theatrical stage, and I'm not likely to.* That may be true. However, whether or not you've ever belted out a song or "shuffled off to Buffalo," I do believe you have been invited to play a key role in Jesus's narrative. You've been given a place to shine, a place of influence. A stage on which to stand, and a light to find.

Now, before I get shouted down, let me tell you what I'm not talking about: I'm not talking about stages that pander to fame and notoriety. (Though God can and regularly does use both for his own renown.) I'm not talking about one-woman showcases for pride, pedigree, or position. I'm not talking about a well-lit place for our ego to lick its wounds or to get its strokes. And I'm certainly not talking theatrical razzle-dazzle where we spackle over every imperfection or weakness, sing and dance our hearts out, and pray that, if nothing else, the applause will somehow make the exhausting performance worth it. Stages that we use to illicitly fill the places only Jesus can; where we live our lives to be noticed by others; where we plaster on a brave face, though the truth of our lives is something quite different—none of those stages, though tempting, will ever produce the kind of kingdom adventures our hearts are starved to taste.

The kind of stages I want to tour with you are the stages God has given you—stages made from passion and built on purpose. They're God-ordained. *God-stages are those specific places where Jesus has called you to bravely enter into the story he is telling and to inhabit your role fully.* They are places where he calls us to enter, willing to be known as we are. Brokenness and brilliance? Beauty and blight? Bring it all. A God-stage is where we can drop the brave act and pick up authentic bravery—born of Jesus himself. It's a place of faith where we reengage with Jesus after years of sidelining ourselves, fear loosening its chokehold on our hearts as we do. A God-stage is where we reclaim the joy of stepping into the story God has specifically called us to, not longing for somebody else's, but fully embracing our own story with Jesus. And finally, a God-stage is the place where we can risk it all, going "all in," because if eternity is as real as we proclaim on Sunday mornings, why wouldn't we? Why wouldn't we "leave it all on the stage" as performers are fond of saying?

If we will dare to take the stage, the Jericho walls around our hearts will start quaking. What has long been asleep will wake. Marooned dreams will raise the sail again. And some form of these brave words will find their way out of our mouths: "This is eternally important. It's worth my time. This story is beyond bigger than me, but I am called to play a role in it. By grace, God has ushered me to this stage, to shine in his light, and I'm going to do so until he tells me it's time to leave the scene and exit the stage."

One Stage Does Not Fit All

Proscenium. Black box. In-the-round. These are just a few types of the different stages used in the theater world. They're all unique, and because of that, they all require unique ways of presenting theatrical material. The heart-stopping music of *Les Misérables* would be staged differently depending on whether it was being presented in the round (audience members on all sides), or on a proscenium stage (traditional theater), or in a black box theater (simple, square-shaped). The kind of stage an actor works on changes everything about the work the actor does.

In the same way, our God-stages can and should look amazingly different from one another. This is no one-size-fits-all God we're talking about; he's endlessly creative. One woman's stage is not another's. And I'm thankful for that, because if I tried to stand on your stage, in your light, I'd be doing so in my own gumption and not by the empowering grace of Christ. And the results would be something far less than what we are truly aching for. He doesn't call us to stand on someone else's stage any more than he calls us to stand in someone else's shadow. Ultimately our stages are as creative and as colorful as the God who calls us to stand upon them.

Your particular stage may be that opulently lit boardroom where it's time to raise some uncomfortable questions. Or perhaps it's your annual candlelit Christmas dinner, where your teenaged son announces that he no longer believes in Jesus. Your stage may be under the streetlight where you tell a fragile woman that her life really doesn't have to be that way. Maybe it is where you rise up under those fluorescent lights and bravely spit out the pain of a secret addiction that has kept you in prison for more years than you care to count.

Different stages. Different audiences. Different results. Not one stage more stunning than the other. Not one more necessary. Not one more effective. The kingdom needs them all.

Audience of Few

Once upon a time, in the land of ancient Persia, a young beauty stood upon a peculiar stage, playing the starring role in an epic drama, with consequences that reach all the way to you and me. And she did all this essentially for an audience of very few: the king and his attendants. Her peculiar stage? The smooth marbled floors of the king's inner court. Her costume? The Bible says this beauty was decked out, likely in a formal gown. Her lines? Not one word. Zip. Zilch. At least at first. Her light? Perhaps she sauntered onto her stage by the glare of the noonday sun or crept in by the flickering glow of evening torches. Whether by day or night, we're not told. But what we are told is that this young woman entered a scene she had not been invited to (by anyone, except God), placing her life and the lives of her people, the Jews, into the hands of the One who sent her.

Behind the political scene of the day, a near sociopathic character named Haman had turned his evil eye toward the total annihilation of her people, the Jewish nation. The wheels of destruction were turning, and only an intervention at the highest level would stop them. Enter our girl. All eyes on her, she waited without one word, willing to be scrutinized, risking life and limb to play her part in the grand Story. Whatever the potential cost, this young woman knew that she had been made "for such a time as this" (Esther 4:14). And she understood that being made "for such a time as this" meant acting. Doing. Risking. She stood in her light, as the king actually applauded her risky act, asking her what she wanted him to do for her. And when the king asked, she opened her mouth and spit it out. Her willingness to speak changed everything. The Jewish people were spared as a result of her bravery: the very people from whom Jesus would spring. Evil would hang from its own gallows, and years later Jerusalem would rise from ruin. All because one young woman dared to take the stage God was giving her.

Our leading lady's name, as you may have guessed, is Queen Esther. Esther, whose name, ironically, means "star." Star, indeed.

Though it seems difficult to believe when we're stuck between the grind of Monday and the grounding of Sunday, this eternal truth remains: we have been called to bravely take the God-stages of our lives no less than Queen Esther. We serve the same God, and he isn't finished telling his story to a desperate world.

Crowd or king? Widely seen or barely noticed? Standing ovation or rotten tomatoes? We have to leave the outcomes and reviews to the Father of lights. That is his part, and his part alone. Our part is to step up and show up, readying ourselves to take the stage with Jesus in the divine Drama . . . and the rest, the glorious rest, is up to him.

drama or Drama?

There are two distinct kinds of drama that I'd like to throw some light on. One is authentic, the other counterfeit. One is all "show"; the other is all substance. And though both are called "drama," they are as different from one another as millennials and baby boomers.

Breathe the word "drama" to just about anyone and you'll probably get a bit of a sideways look. Maybe the same expression as that wincing, all-teeth emoji. "She's such a drama queen." "You're not going to believe the drama." "Drama mama."

I think you get the picture. "Little d" drama—*drama* from here on out—is chaos-creation and overreaction. It's commotion instead of calm. It's freak-out instead of finesse. Splash a little water and the drama queen will swear a tsunami has occurred. Sadly, *drama* lovers leave people spun and fried; they constantly borrow trouble, and they usually burn through relationships faster than a match.

Several years ago, during a disorienting low in my life, I found myself sucked in by *drama*. A key relationship had been strained to the point of rupture, and my battle with insomnia had returned with an ax to grind, leaving me up to do—what else? Watch TV. And before I knew it, I was a captive audience to one of those reality shows that simply bleeds *drama*. The characters were constantly at odds with one another, tossing verbal jabs or "throwing shade," as it is often called. Though there was nothing bleep-worthy, the show was a dark antithesis to one of my favorite Scriptures, "Every good and perfect gift is from above, coming down from the Father of the heavenly lights, with whom there is no change or shifting shadow" (James 1:17 BSB).

Yet, before I knew it, I was hooked. I knew it wasn't okay. To watch on TV what I would never abide in real life? Madness. But *drama* doesn't appeal to reason; it appeals to the swirl, to the hot mess, to the adrenaline hit of fight-or-flight emotion. It reflected outwardly something I was experiencing inwardly. After a while, however, I started to wake up feeling vaguely sick, like I had a low-grade *drama* fever. I had little energy for kingdom things; all my fight had been spent watching one too many brawls in a silly "reality" show. When I finally turned the TV off and began to scoot a little closer to the Redeemer of my heart, I heard his gentle, but firm, "Come back to me, Allison." It's as if he was saying to me, "You were made to shine, and in ways you don't even know, *drama* is dulling that shine." I quickly caught his drift. I was existing like the people of Israel spoken of in Isaiah, who were "living in the land of deep darkness" (9:2). But, like them, I was being invited back into "a great light." I was being invited back to participate in the real deal, the genuine thing. Something so illustrious that it requires a capital *D*.

Capital *D* Drama

Arise, shine, for your light has come. (Isa. 60:1a)

In the same way, let your light shine before others, that they may see your good works and give glory to your Father who is in heaven. (Matt. 5:16 ESV)

Do everything without complaining or arguing, so that you may be blameless and pure, children of God without fault in a crooked and depraved generation—in which you **shine like stars** *in the universe—as you hold out the word of life.* (Phil. 2:14–15, paraphrase, emphasis mine)

Do these words cause a rising inside you? Have you leaning forward in your chair? Releasing a long-stifled spiritual roar? If so, then you're encountering capital *D* Drama—God's eternal narrative, and the God-given role you and I play in it. This is Drama, the way God meant us to experience it. God's living Word overflows the margins with astonishingly active derring-do, with life-and-death charges, many of which have our names on them; which is as it should be, because at the essence of the word "drama" lies its Greek root—*drān*—which means "to act or to do."[2]

Long before the word meant an emotional performance or became the recipe of reality TV, "drama" meant to do something significant in the story being told. It meant to face conflict. It meant gutsy, decisive choice. It meant to act. That's essentially why someone who acts is called an actress or an actor.

In many ways, God himself was the prototypical actor on the messed-up scene of humankind. Onto that Genesis garden stage he entered, back when we were playing hide-and-go-seek behind fig-leaf costumes. There, God sought us out, spoke to our fearfully sinful hearts, and set ultimate redemption in motion because he was intent on the eternal Drama of doing and acting on our behalf. Because if he didn't intervene—if the God of the universe didn't *do something* dramatic—you and I and everyone we love were going to go on choosing for ourselves, making broken choice after broken choice for all eternity. We would never reenter Eden—not on earth, nor in eternity. We needed Someone to step in. We needed Someone to speak for us. Someone to change the course of the inevitably broken way things were going. Someone to make a way where there was no way. In other words, Someone to act. Henry Miller says it this way: "The ordinary man is involved in action, the hero acts. An immense difference."[3]

Boy, did God our hero act, setting in motion capital *D* Drama, the likes of which will continue until time itself ceases. This redemptive Drama will play on until the Director says, "Time for time's final bow. Bring down the curtain." But until that moment, you and I, as followers of Jesus, are compelled to act, to do, to take the stage with him.

Are you ready to take the stage with Jesus?

Encore

So maybe you're wondering what happened to the folded-up girl in the California parking lot.

Here's what I wish had happened: I wish I'd magically rallied, telling the panic attack it could heel, like an ill-behaved dog, under the scrubby California bush, because I had things to do and a stage to take with Jesus. I wish the fear had buckled its knee and loosed its chokehold on my chest as I valiantly recalled every scriptural promise regarding fear's defeat. I wish some bystander had swooped in with a reassuring word, giving me the most Hollywoodesque, locker room, bash-this-bully speech ever known to woman. I wish, somehow, I'd put on the brave act and gotten on the stage with a wing and prayer anyway.

But this wasn't the movies. This wasn't magic. This was just regular old, wrecked me.

I walked up to my friend—the friend who had brought me in—looking like I'd survived an emotional tsunami, and

I think she knew. We talked for a moment, and by the end of that moment, she mentioned her concern about not having enough time to properly run through all the technical elements for the drama to be as strong as it could be. She let me off the hook without telling me she was letting me off the hook. She was a lot like Jesus in that moment.

I recall little else of the conference that year, except feeling like a walking wrung-out washcloth everywhere I went. I thought everyone could see my mess. The white-hot panic had gone but had left regret and shame in its wake. As shame researcher Dr. Brene Brown so perfectly states, "Shame is the most powerful, master emotion. It's the fear that we're not good enough."[4] I certainly felt like I wasn't good enough. Not even living in the same neighborhood. Honestly, I was grateful when I could fly back to the rolling hills of Tennessee and forget the whole thing.

So imagine my surprise when the event invited me back—the very next year—to do the very same piece—in the very same place. Imagine my surprise when I was given a second chance. Imagine my surprise when I heard my own voice say *yes* and I boarded a plane to fly across the country back to the scene of panic's crime. Imagine what it felt like to stand on the stage—the one I had not been able to take just the year before—as the piece went off without a hitch and seemed to hit the hearts of the conference attendees in ways I never could've predicted and had only ever hoped for.

Through that painful and redemptive experience, Jesus was saying some things to my heart—and maybe to your heart as well:

Hey, child, do you think I only call you once upon a time? Just one time and one time only, and if you blow it, well then, tough luck? This isn't about a perfect show. It's not about putting on the perfect act. Perfect isn't even possible where you are. Watch, and I'll make far more use of your consecrated weaknesses than I will ever make of your "perfected" strengths.

In the capital *D* Drama I'm inviting you to, it's all about the Great Again. It's about getting back up. Believing. Risking. Again. Taking the stage with me, again, even if you've had some knocks along the way. I am your Great Light, kid, and I've got a place for that light to shine. You're a lamp on a stand, giving light to everyone in the house. And that light cannot be snuffed out, because its source is me.

Remember, I don't call you once upon a time. I call you time after time after time. And I will never stop.

God had graciously given me a spiritual encore, and it changed my life forever.

Sparkler: Fellow sojourner, in which areas have you suffered from spiritual stage fright? How long has it been since you've dared to step from the shadows? In what ways do you believe you've been invited to play a role in the divine Drama of God? What are some specific ways you have settled for its counterfeit—*drama*?

2

The Brave Act
and Character Shoes

How beautiful on the mountains are the feet of
those who bring good news.

Isaiah 52:7

Dropping the Brave Act

When the clamor quiets inside—which is not nearly often
enough these days—I sometimes hear Jesus whispering the
same enticing thing he first said to me when I was all of nineteen years of age, sporting a deeply unnecessary spiral-rod
perm. "There is so much more for you, beloved, than acting
your way through life. Feel free to embrace the rest of realness. Feel free to drop the brave act anytime."

Feel free to drop the brave act? That's a pretty audacious thing to say to an actor.

Even then, I knew those words were an invitation and a map for shedding the façade of bravery I had donned like an ill-fitting costume and putting on the authentic bravery Jesus held in his beautiful hands.

In short, Jesus was encouraging me to save the playacting for the stage. He had gifted me with it there. "How about leaving it there?" he seemed to be asking. Jesus was offering me the rest of realness—in real life, where it mattered.

Through one of his characters in *The Screwtape Letters*, C. S. Lewis puts it this way: "When He [God] talks of their losing their selves, He only means abandoning the clamour of self-will; once they have done that, He [God] *actually gives them back all their personality*, and boasts . . . that when *they are wholly His they will be more themselves than ever.*"[1]

Daily, Jesus holds out this wild and genuine offer. Yet for me, in some ways the battle for authentic, Jesus-soaked realness is just as fraught as it was when I was a green-as-they-come Brat Pack wannabe, hoping for a career in the theater.

Acting in the Eighties

When I arrived at Carnegie Mellon University to study acting in the fashion-forward decade of the 1980s—1988 to be exact—I came ready to act. Not just on the stage, but off it. I steeled myself against what I knew would be unreal competitiveness—Carnegie Mellon was, and still is, one of the most difficult acting conservatories to get into. And to graduate from. During the years that I attended, only about half of the fifty or so students who were admitted actually graduated. At the time, Carnegie Mellon operated a notorious cut system, culling weaker students left and right.

Better be tough. Better be brilliant. Better be brave. Because if you weren't, you would be eaten alive by the system and by your own insidious insecurity. So, daily, like blue eyeliner and leg warmers, I put my brave on. When some of the other students subtly mentioned people they had studied with, the scholarships they had won to pay for CMU's hefty price tag, the callbacks they were scoring, I tried to join in, acting as if I, too, were numbered in their throng. Color me brave, brilliant, and tough. Me too, by goodness. Me too.

But no matter how much I tried to "woman up," I felt like a fraud. No matter how much I spackled on my best "brave act," the truth of the matter was that I felt out of my depth and out of my league; I was scared to death, and acting to the contrary off the stage was exhausting me. I lived in a perpetual state of fight or flight, vigilant to defend myself against my pooling insecurity. The 24/7 performer, layering act upon act. In many ways I had become a better actor off the stage than I ever had been on.

And Jesus wanted to do something about that.

The Circle That Changed Everything

On opening night of most shows, before the houselights dim and the curtain rises on the show's eye-catching opening moment, an onstage circle is forming. "Circle up!" the stage manager or director will often call. If it's not a virulent flu season, actors and available techies oblige, sometimes joining hands. An unbroken circle takes shape as the director gives final instruction and encouragement for the work at hand. Usually what needs to be said boils down to this: Trust the work. Trust one another.

The circle that changed everything for me looked a bit different. As a freshman I had been cast as a chorus member in a student director's reimagined, 1970s-esque Greek tragedy. Being a part of the show as a freshman was, in and of itself, a little unusual, because at CMU one generally didn't perform until junior year. Being cast, however, was no great testament to my outsized talent but to my outsized size. The women were supposed to look somewhat Amazonian—and since I roll at five feet twelve inches in bare feet, I possessed the requisite Amazonian stature in spades.

I looked at myself in the dressing room—in my crazed discotheque attire and my funky hoop earrings, thinking, *I'm done for now. I'll mess up standing still and holding my picket sign. They'll see what a fraud I am. How I don't belong here. How they chose the wrong girl. I'm done for.* I distinctly remember the barrage of personal lack. Willing on my best brave face, I stood up from the chair and, ironically, started acting all the way to the stage.

"Allison? Allison." Someone was calling my name. I turned and squinted into the dark hall. It took me a second to recognize that it was April, a storied upperclassman. In our world, any upperclassman was storied, because it meant they had dodged the blades of "the cut" as it was known to everyone in the drama program. I immediately wondered if April needed me to fetch something for her—a bobby pin or eyelash glue. But she didn't seem to want anything from me—except for me to come closer. I moved with the haste of an underclassman, bending down a bit to hear the strange words she was saying.

"Hey, Allison, listen, um, some of us like to . . . ya know, pray before we do shows. Some of us in the department are Christians, and we thought you might want to pray with us." I don't remember what I said in response to April, except an automatic "of course," as I followed her to some hidden cranny of the small theater. Turning a corner, I happened upon four or five acting students who welcomed me with authentic warmth. I remember thinking, *Why me?* One of them stretched out a hand. I placed my nervous palm in it as we all gripped hands, and the tiny, secret circle formed. The prayers commenced, and, though I know many words were uttered—I even know they prayed for me—to this day, it was the name of Jesus that received star billing. I had never heard his name spoken the way these brave young guns said it. At least, not in the theater. It was as if they knew he was *really with them*. Even in the pressure cooker of the conservatory experience.

In that circle something miraculous began to gestate inside me. After a dry prodigal season, brittle belief found rain. Countless seeds that good people had scattered for years on the soil of my life began to break open. When I accepted the invitation into that holy circle and heard people my own age, of my own odd "tribe," intoning a name that I had known and once loved, my heart turned toward wholeness. It was there that I first heard the clarion call of Jesus, issuing that enticing invitation I was bending your ear about at the beginning of this chapter:

"Child, are you ready to drop the brave act? Are you ready for the rest of realness?"

A Pair of Shoes and the Truth

A few months before I joined that hallowed circle, I had moved into Carnegie Mellon University's Donner Hall, lugging boxes that brimmed with the evidence of my small-town Carolina life. Bringing all the things a semi-normal acting student might—boyfriend mixtapes, journals of overly earnest babble, and more clean, white underwear than should be legal—my family and I stacked boxes in the corner.

There was, however, one box that stood out from the pack—my theater box. In it I packed unitards and leg warmers, reams of sheet music and monologues, and a tackle box full of pancake makeup. Oh. And a very specific pair of shoes—a pair that I would use onstage for nearly twenty years.

They're called "character shoes."

Bring to mind the most utilitarian, simply-strapped, low-heeled (usually black) shoe in your closet, and you'd come close to imagining what a character shoe looks like. A character shoe is a sturdy walking shoe. A grown-up shoe. If you saw a picture of a character shoe in an Instagram feed, you'd think: Down. Right. Homely.

But those homely-looking character shoes are not as boring as they might seem at first glance. If you could turn character shoes sideways, they would give up their insider secrets. Character shoes are often bracketed (outfitted with reinforcing steel) at the arch, so the heel doesn't snap off onstage.

They sometimes sport rubberized soles, so that no moment-marring slippage happens. The no-slip feature is most handy when you are hoofin' it on a sweat-dabbled stage or raising the emotive roof with those high notes.

Whatever the character, no musical theater gal worth her salt would be caught sans her character shoes. Think of a drummer and drumsticks. A chef and knives. Any human being (that has one) and their phone. Character shoes are part and parcel of an actor's craft.

I suspect in the almost one thousand times I have played some type of character onstage—from my auspicious beginnings as a kindergarten bovine all the way through to performing the hand jive approximately 650 times on Broadway in the mid-1990s revival of *Grease*—I have donned my trusty character shoes, or a pair very much like them, every time.

At Carnegie, as young actors in training we were encouraged by our credentialed professors to be prepared for anything—especially any unexpected audition opportunity. For me, that usually meant dragging around a duffel bag full of dancewear, headshots/résumés, and those ubiquitous character shoes.

We all lived for that ol' audition magic when a director liked us well enough to give us a callback, which meant we had made it past the initial cut. I can recall many a dance captain calling, "Okay. Time to dance! No marking the choreography—let's have the steps full-out."

We buckled our character shoes snugly and proceeded to perform our hearts out, praying that we were the perfect fit for whatever role they happened to be casting. Character shoes are nondescript and utilitarian—made to fit any type of character we needed to play. Character shoes are built to keep the show going. Whoever we were needed to be we *could* be if we were wearing our trusty character shoes. We could play anyone in them. Anyone.

If only I'd saved them for the stage.

Here's a spotlight truth: the invitation to realness that Jesus issued in the Pittsburgh prayer circle would take me years to fully comprehend. It took some considerable time to recognize that I had lived entire chunks of my life in character shoes, starting in adolescence. I lived my life—on more days than not—with a twisty loop running through my head: *Tell me who you want me to be, and I'll be that. Tell me what character I have to play, and I'll play it to the hilt.* Even when I bolted back to Jesus in the theater that night, I did so in character shoes. Honestly, I didn't know any other way of being. Being "just me" was a terrifying proposition. Character shoes assured me that I could be anyone but myself. Anything but real. I marched those puppies straight into the kingdom and right on into church, without missing a bit of choreography, ready to play the day's character. Ready to play whatever part I had to in order to be accepted.

Gregarious greeter? On go the character shoes.

Intense intercessor? On go the character shoes.

Effective evangelizer? On go the character shoes.

Now, of course, there's absolutely nothing wrong with any of those functions or positions, especially if God has called and equipped a gal for them. But they weren't authentic to me. They were characters that I put on. I kept right on dancing and acting offstage—playing whatever character I thought would bring me acceptance. I was the embodiment of a performance-based believer. I lived life like I was in the hunt for the role of a lifetime. After all, I was living my life in character shoes, right? I could be most anybody at anytime. And "dropping character"—a cardinal sin in the theater world—was out of the question, because once a character is assumed, you never let the real person underneath peek through. I was trapped inside myself. My character shoes were superglued to my feet (and heart) for huge portions of my life in Christ.

I meet women all the time—passionate, mature Christ chasers—who are exhausted from staying in character all the time, even in church. Sometimes especially in church. The effort it takes to "be someone else" feels Herculean. Often we are worn out before we ever enter the building, amping ourselves up for our performance. We become experts at figuring out who we have to be, what "character" we have to play in order to be accepted.

Certain ways of acting, certain personalities are elevated. Others are not. Certain types of experience, certain types of language are accepted. Others are not. And we women are pretty smart cookies—usually we can discern what "types" or "characters" are likely to get us included in the next coffee klatch. Studies tell us that social rejection can be as painful as a lingering physical wound.[2] Most of us would do anything to avoid it, and so if playing a role keeps us as part of the "big show" or makes our place in the "big show" more understandable, then we'll play it. Because often, playing a character feels safer to us than daring to be ourselves without props and masks. Often we'd rather act ourselves to exhaustion and fit in rather than be ourselves and risk rejection.

The Red Character Shoes

Remember an old movie called the *The Red Shoes*? The plot boils down to a girl at the ballet in a tragic search for love, destined to dance no matter the price. It's all about those red shoes. Even though some slightly more romanticized versions exist in film and onstage, Hans Christian Andersen's original fairy tale contains a much darker picture of what happens when a woman becomes trapped in shoes that aren't exactly what they seem.

Andersen's "once upon a time" goes like so: Karen, an orphan, has been given a rough pair of red shoes by her mother. Karen is, by all accounts, beautiful, but possesses a selfish streak as wide as the Mississippi River, ever ungrateful for what she does have. Karen is adopted by a wealthy woman and is given a beautiful pair of red silken shoes, of which she becomes very proud. The normal otherworldy twists and turns occur in Andersen's fairy tale, until Karen finally becomes possessed by her shoes. She does not control them; they control her. They are always moving, taking her places she would rather not go. Karen is being danced to death by her shoes.

Tormented, she tries everything to remove them, to no avail. Ultimately, she cuts off her own feet to rid herself of the constant controlling movement. Maimed for life, Karen tries to enter the church for respite and restoration and finds that her own amputated feet, still in the red shoes, bar the way to the house of God. This happens over and over again, until she quits trying to go to the house of God and prays for an angel to deliver her to heaven.[3]

Atrocious? Absolutely.

Accurate? More than I'd like to admit.

Shoes that control. Shoes that bar a real experience in God's house. Sounds an awful lot like the character shoes I wore for much of my life. I'm finding that I'm not alone in that. Perhaps you know the feeling too.

Cornering the Character

She was a leader in the church. As she bear-hugged her women good-bye after the event, it was obvious that they felt she could rope the moon, if given a long enough lasso.

As we began to chat, I mentally described her: Astute. Aspirational. Articulate. I admit I found myself thinking, *Does she moonlight as a model?*

Then she swallowed hard before she gave up her bruised heart: "I wear character shoes, Allison. Just like what you spoke about. Most every day. So much is demanded of me in the role of pastor's wife, and I can't carry the weight of their expectations. I love Christ. I treasure the call on my husband's life. And I love the women." She smiled and confessed, "The truth is, I'm desperately depressed. I have been for almost a year. I can't play the character of the perfect pastor's wife anymore. It's too much."

The first choice we must make when stepping into a bigger kingdom story is to recognize the characters we play—acknowledging that, yes, those are character shoes on my feet. In my own life, recognition has been half the battle. I see you, character shoes.

Maybe your character is the "unflappable mom." Maybe your character is the "insecure friend." Maybe your character is the "wisdom woman." Maybe your character is the "avoider." Maybe your character is "perfect ministry leader." When we recognize the false character roles we play—the ones that indenture us, the ones that drain us of vitality—then we can begin to let them go.

Reassuring the Role-Player

I don't think most Christian women play a character because they are hiding some deep secret. *I'm going to play the role of the perfect wife/business woman/team member/ Christian worker because, if I don't, my double life as an international embezzler will be discovered.* I don't think it goes anything like that. I'm sure that on occasion a dark double-life is being hidden, but personally, I have yet to meet a believing woman doing a one-woman Jekyll and Hyde show in her own life.

I think most of us don character shoes because we are desperately trying to do whatever we think will secure our acceptance with whatever group we happen to find ourselves frequenting. We learn well—sometimes starting in childhood—how to be the kind of person who always seems to be included or thought well of. So we try her "type" on. And when it works, when we get those first heady hits of affirmation, we keep putting "her" on, not understanding that we've adopted a character. The playacting sneaks up on us, until we discover we've become mimics of someone else. All in an effort to belong.

Yet no mimicry is necessary in the body of Christ. Not when we're made for so much more. Blessedly, we don't have to wear ourselves out trying to fit in with the clique, when we already belong in the kingdom.[4] We already have a seat with Jesus in heavenly places (Eph. 1:20). In Jesus, we already belong. First John 4:4a boils it down to a beautiful stanza: "Little children, you belong to God" (ISV). We belong. In Christ, we've already been picked. We've already been chosen. We're already accepted in the beloved. We don't have to strive for something that is already ours.

When we allow Jesus to reassure our internal character actor with the truth that we belong, we discover a freedom that is rare and exhilarating. And as scary as this new freedom can feel emotionally, it's actually the doorway to the glorious freedom Christ promises.

The Gift of a Poor Fit

From time to time, I am asked to present a shortened version of my teaching on character shoes. For one event, I practiced rigorously at home, whittling the piece down to its allotted five minutes. On my final rehearsal, I was struck by what I just *knew* would be a stroke of storytelling brilliance! It would be the froth on the whole cappuccino. I approached a nearby stool, sat down, crossed a leg, and tried to cram my foot into my old character shoes—the pair I have owned for over twenty-five years. I tried several different angles, trying to squeeze my foot into the shoe, hoping I could get it on and finish out my vignette with a well-placed time-step! There was only one problem.

The shoe didn't fit anymore.

When I had last worn the character shoes, I was a size 8½. And there I was, firmly a size 10—thanks to my late-in-life miracle, Luke the Red (my five-year-old), and the hard-to-lose perimenopausal mother-of-a-preschooler weight he had gifted me with. I'm sure I looked a little like Cinderella's cray-cray stepsisters, who, in the official version of the fairy tale, sawed off their ten little piggies to fit the glass slipper. They were so desperate to play a role that was not theirs to play, to have Cinderella's story, if you will, that they chose a maimed and crippled life rather than giving up the ill-fitting shoe.

After I stopped cramming a too-little character shoe with a too-big foot, I thought, *That's right, Lord. That's right. New wine cannot be poured into old wineskins. The old wineskins will burst. The old simply cannot contain the new things that you have done, Jesus. Thank you that what was once so comfortable no longer fits.*

Though I never found the perfect closing moment for my character shoes vignette, I discovered something far better: I discovered the gift of a poor fit. Because even if I forget—even if I somehow manage to shove the new, bursting activity of Jesus into a tiny ol' character shoe—even if I start acting in real life again—I won't be able to walk for long. How do I know when I'm sporting character shoes? Exhaustion is my first clue, and if I continue, I will be faced with a painful rub that will blister at warp speed. Soon, I will be hobbled. And that pain is a gift for people like me.

The pain forces me to pay attention to what's not working. It's an indicator that my internal actor is wreaking havoc again, trying to step into the spotlight. When I feel the exhaustion and the rub, I stop. I look down. I examine the shoes I'm wearing and switch them out for ones that set my feet free.

Sparkler: Do you believe you belong in the kingdom? Why or why not? In what area of your life do you feel pressure to keep up appearances? Which parts of your life, if any, do you spend in character shoes? What steps can you take to put them aside for the real you?

3

Ancient Character Shoes

It is God who arms me with strength
   and keeps my way secure.
He makes my feet like the feet of a deer;
   he causes me to stand on the heights.
He trains my hands for battle.

Psalm 18:32–34a

I bet a batch of artisanal bacon-infused maple syrup that most of us who grew up in church learned the story of David and Goliath. David and those five smooth stones. I think you could also call it "David and the temptation of character shoes."

Imagine the scene: Israel has a big-time bully on its hands. For forty days and nights, Bully Goliath and his crew hurl

vicious insults at the people of God, asking for someone—
anyone—to man up and bring the heat. No one on the Israelite
side will step up and be the nation's stand-up guy.

Young David is sent to the standoff by his pop, Jesse,
armed with vittles for his older brothers, who are soldiers
on Team Israel. David, who scholars believe was about
thirteen or fourteen at the time, hears all the hubbub and
tosses out, "I don't know who you think you are, Goliath—
you and your impressively vertical self—but you are dealing
with the favorite kids of the Most High God, and you're
about to eat dust." Saul hears the boast and is impressed.
Hey, if no one else can topple this dude, might as well let
the kid try.

The Bible picks up the narrative with these words about
King Saul's armor: "So Saul clothed David with his armor,
and he put a bronze helmet on his head; he also clothed him
with a coat of mail. David fastened his sword to his armor
and tried to walk, for he had not tested them. And David
said to Saul, 'I cannot walk with these, for I have not tested
them.' So David took them off" (1 Samuel 17:38–39 NKJV).

So. He. Took. Them. Off.

Usually we breeze right past that phrase, rushing ahead to
where David uses the giant's colossal forehead as a bull's-eye.
However, I believe those five words just might be the most
potent in all of young David's emerging story. Could it be
that the reason David had the wherewithal to stand against
Goliath is contained in those five simple words?

So. He. Took. Them. Off.

Scholars tell us that with multiplied thousands watching
from the wings, David, an adolescent boy, took off King

Saul's weaponry and said, "No, thank you, King Saul. I'm sorry, this simply will not get the job done. I don't know your weapons. Your very shiny and impressive sword and your heavy, impenetrable armor have not been proven trustworthy to me. I didn't protect my father's flocks with sword and armor. I protected them with bare hands, stones, and a slingshot. What's more, I can't move in these things, no matter how shiny they are. They don't fit me. Respectfully, King Saul, no thank you."[1]

Don't miss it. King Saul's weapons (which you and I might imagine as an ancient version of character shoes)

- weren't known to David,
- didn't fit him, and
- made it utterly impossible to move.

That's a rock-solid list to determine whether you might be trying to trample your own giants in character shoes. Do you go to spiritual war with weapons you don't know? Young David relied on the true and tested weapons of his warfare: five stones and a slingshot. Night after night he learned to launch the stone against the forehead of any wily thing attacking the flock he shepherded. David could trust those weapons. What weapons has God made strong in your solitude? What weapons do you know intimately? Look to those and trust them. They will hold in the day of battle.

Do you go to war in things that don't fit? Had David tried to tackle Goliath in Saul's armor, David likely would have tripped and rolled his way into the valley, ending up a heap of tangled metal at Goliath's unpedicured feet. After all, we know that King Saul was a tall man, and David was just a boy. The ill-fitting armor wouldn't have helped David—not in the least. In fact, it would have hindered him from reaching his destiny. No wonder David exclaims, "I cannot walk!" before he courageously sheds this ancient version of character shoes. He would be David in the conflict and no one else.[2] He would go to war as himself.

I won't pretend it's easy to say "no thanks" to character shoes. It's not. Scholars tell us that thousands were gathered around the Elah Valley as David made his decision. Thousands of judgmental looks. Thousands of dismissive grunts. How in the world do you say "no thank you" to a king? Especially when the armor and weapons are so impressive that anyone would be honored to wear them.

You do it by having faith that sometimes saying "no thank you" to the good opens the door for the better. Sometimes saying "no thank you" to the king's weapons will open the door to watching your God-given weapons slay the giant. The first great step of faith is believing that what Jesus has entrusted to you is enough.

Taking off the character shoes is the first step toward a life of incredible shine.

Personal Goliaths and Someone Else's Weapons

For a long time I tried to fight spiritual battles clutching someone else's weapons; it was akin to wearing someone else's ill-fitting—albeit beautiful—costume in a show. Whenever a particularly nasty giant would rear its terrifying head,

I would speak to myself like this: *Well, this is a bugaboo. This situation is gonna devour my morning bagel if I don't get in the game. Come on, Allen. Time to pull out the big gun of intercession.*

After giving myself a good talking-to, I would hide in my closet and decide I wasn't coming out until whatever giant lurking around my life was eating dust and I was standing on its proverbial neck. My spiritual teeth were cut on passionate preaching that elevated intense, hours-long intercession as a superlative gift. Many folks I knew wanted to be an intercessor. So, I decided: I would intercede that thing down if it killed me.

There was only one problem with that strategy, and it happened to be a rather sticky one: I don't have the gift of intercession. I pray, of course; I have been led at points in my life to pray for extended times. But those were seasons divinely directed and enabled. As a whole, on any given day, lengthy intercession is not my go-to weapon or spiritual tool. In fact, I'm nothing like the intercessors I personally know who feel divinely empowered to bear prayer burdens that might break others' spiritual backs.

My own mother-in-law, Jetta, is called to and gifted in intercession and for years has "stood in the gap" when I take a stage to speak. I respect Jetta's gift, and to be honest, I have often longed to be likewise gifted. But whenever I've decided to "put on" intercession—a spiritual weapon that I don't truly know and that I couldn't "move in" with freedom—well, that is akin to my going to battle in King Saul's clothing. That is my version of putting on spiritual character shoes. It doesn't quite fit.

So how in the world is a gal supposed to take off her own character shoes and whip an overgrown spiritual bully? A couple of years ago I found out.

A Custom-Fit Weapon

Ever experience a spiritual body blow? You snooze the alarm on what seems to be a garden-variety day and find your legs have been unexpectedly swept from under you. One of those days almost did me in. This day's blow was one of the more terrifying giant bullies I've ever faced. It affected everything—my demeanor, my way of relating to my husband (who is as good as the day is long, mind you), even my desire to stay engaged in day-to-day life. It felt as if the life I had been nestled in had burned down to ash, and that ash had been blown away by a wicked wind. To make matters far worse, I largely went silent on the whole thing.

In time my unhealed silence turned into seething. And my seething gave way to something more devastating than the event that caused it—unforgiveness. What had started out as an acorn of anger became an oak of unforgiveness.

This went on for the better part of a year and a half. I was coming dangerously close to the state that Hebrews 12:15 describes: "Be careful that no one falls short of the grace of God, so that no root of bitterness will spring up to cause trouble and defile many" (BSB).

I knew I was in trouble, largely because any time the word *unforgiveness* was mentioned, I would bristle internally, which gave me all the evidence I needed that I had a giant squatter in my life. Somewhere in Goliath's brutal residency,

I woke to another "normal" day of bitter frustration—except something about that morning felt different. I had the sense that there were places Jesus wanted to take me, but my unforgiveness was blocking the path forward. I had no other choice but to face my Goliath.

I had tried everything I knew to defeat my personal giant—especially the weapon of intercession. I remember running up to my closet that day, deciding I would intercede unforgiveness out of my life for good. I ran out of words in about ten minutes. My praying felt religious, forced, and feeble.

After I had worn myself out trying on somebody else's weaponry, I moved from the closet to the kitchen. I still sensed that God was insistently nudging. *This is your day. The time is now.* And so I simply stood in my kitchen and asked one of the most important questions in my spiritual walk: *Jesus, how? How do I march down into the valley of my own sin and face it? How do I take it down?* I didn't hear an audible voice, but somehow my heart knew what to do.

Filling my lungs to the bottom, I took a breath, raised my shaky hand, and said one word.

Jesus

And then I said it again a little louder.

Jesus

And, finally, finally, after such a silent season: I sang it.

Jesus

And then that one name gave way to a simple song. A melody of worship. A broken song of praise. A worshiping, wayward heart singing, warring her way home.

In some ways, it was like riding a bike; something you never forget. From my earliest 1970s days—from when I thought Jesus was the superhero of *Godspell*—I was a worshiper. I sang "Day by Day" like others sang "Jesus Loves Me." Even today people sometimes tell me, "I saw you in the car." When they have a twinkle in their eyes, I know they have caught me worshiping. (I promise I keep one hand on the wheel.) My husband is a worship pastor, and though my travel schedule rarely allows it, one of my sweetest spots is by his side on Sunday mornings, worshiping. When I say I could go on and on about musical worship, I mean it to the pinkies of my have-been-known-to-dance-like-David feet.

So that day, facing the giant, I finally did what I have always done. I deployed the weapon that has been tested and proven trustworthy in the deepest deserts of my life. And that weapon was worship.

I remember leaning against my counter, straining to keep my hand in the air as I finally put back on worship (my weapon—my five stones), leaving intercession (someone else's weapon—Saul's sword) to those called to it.

And it was that day, my friend, that my giant blinked first, and began to weeble-wobble.

Want to know what happens when the real you finally shows up on your God-given scene? Giants blink and then they fall. Just like they did for David.

Then he took his staff in his hand, chose five smooth stones . . . and, with his sling in his hand, approached the Philistine . . . and killed him. (1 Sam. 17:40, 50)

When we do like David, we're one step closer to finding our light. We're getting a sneak peek at those unique places of visibility where we bring glory to the Light of the World.

We're beginning to shine.

Sparkler: How might you need to say "no thank you" to inauthentic weapons? What "spiritual weapons" do you know intimately? What weapons have been proven trustworthy to you in your testing times?

4

What's in a Name?

And the man said to him, "What is your name?"

Genesis 32:27 ERV

The slight gentleman stood on the edges of the event the entire day. Everything about his demeanor whispered "invisible." Though socially timid, he was the first to meet any need. When some set piece required striking (removal from the stage), he was a beat ahead of anyone else on the volunteer crew. Then he would retreat offstage again. This "dash in and disappear" cycle went on for the entire conference.

After the event wrapped and I was getting ready to catch a homeward-bound plane, the man approached me. He white-knuckled something in his hand as his eyes began to flood. In muted suffering he looked at his clenched fist, which seemed to hold the source of his pain. I knew immediately what it was.

During my events I lead women to write down the false names they carry around inside and exchange them for the authentic, truth-soaked names God has for us. (More on that later.) I realized that this precious man had also joined in the exercise and held a name tag in his hand. Whatever name he had carried for life was obviously incredibly painful—so painfully seared on him that he hadn't physically been able to relinquish it. The false name was a part of him, no different from his shoe size or the resting rate of his heart.

I looked at him. He looked at me, eyes brimming. I struggled to find the right words. I knew God was healing the man who lived to help.

Finally, indicating the clenched name tag, I said, "May I have it?"

He searched my face and swallowed hard, pressing down on his lips. Again, I asked, "Sir, may I have it? Please?"

He thought for a moment more as he moved his fist toward me and opened his hand. In his palm lay the name that had held him captive, the name that he believed of himself in his worst and best moments alike. A name that kept him on the edges of his life. A name that doomed him to be a shadow dweller. A name that had kept him from finding his light. A name that kept him from living a Jesus-infused brave life. A name that dulled his shine.

In simple penciled print, the name tag said two words: Convicted Felon.

Names

Names. Stubborn, false, painful names. Such names—like my friend carried—have a way of biting down into the very core of who we are. Like a rabid animal, they lock onto tender places, refusing to lose their hold. We may never speak them aloud. We may try to ignore them. We may repeatedly shove them below the watermark of our lives, trying desperately to drown a thing determined to float. But eventually we must do business with them, or they will keep us in the shadows, on the edges, out of the light.

Why do names exert such power?

What's in a name, after all?

It's a question one of the theater's greatest heroines asks in arguably the theater's most recognizable speech. Accompany me back to ninth-grade English to a particular balcony, if you will. A particular balcony after a particular house party, where a particularly aggressive lovebug has bitten a young girl by the name of Juliet. Speaking to the stars in the open air, Juliet doesn't realize Romeo is hidden below, inhaling every adolescent word.

> *Juliet:*   O Romeo, Romeo! wherefore art thou Romeo?
> *Deny thy father and refuse thy name . . .*
> *'Tis but thy name that is my enemy:*
> Thou art thyself, though not a Montague . . .
> O, *be some other name!*
> *What's in a name?* That which we call a rose
> *By any other name would smell as sweet.*[1]

At first glance, Juliet's balcony speech appears to be a hormone-charged profession of love at first sight. But looking more deeply, as the italicized phrases hopefully demonstrate, the recurring theme of Juliet's speech is the inescapable power of a name. In fact, this soliloquy's most famous line is that theme—the power of a name—boiled down.

Romeo, Romeo! wherefore art thou, Romeo?

Now, maybe you're like me. Even after being well taught, even after it was drilled into my teenage brain by fantastic English and drama teachers, for years I thought that particular line meant, "Where art thou, Romeo?"

In other words, "Where in the world are you hiding? Let's end the hide-and-seek game." (After all, Juliet is balcony-bound. They've been separated by more than a little distance, so Romeo could be hiding behind a weeping willow, figuring out how to swoop in for a little lip-lock, right?)

But that interpretation never seemed to make perfect sense. Not in context. Because Juliet is not asking, "Where are you, Romeo?" She is asking, "*Why* are you *Romeo*?" *Wherefore* is an archaic word for "why." In other words, "Why, why, why of all the swoon-worthy boys at the party did I have to fall for a boy named *Romeo*, with the last name of *Montague*?! A family with whom my family has an ongoing grudge match. Why do you possess a name that will always be a gulf between us? Change your name, Romeo, and change our destinies. Be but called R. Masters or R. Marzoni and all will be well."

On that balcony, amidst all the heart-pumping language, Juliet already sees hints of the final tragic act. Her words foreshadow the unstoppable power of warring names—Montague and Capulet—that will always hunt down true love and snuff it out. Even young Juliet recognizes that names are nearly impossible to ditch; she knows names very often determine destiny. And, unfortunately, she's chosen a boy with the wrong name.

What's in a name? More than you ever dreamed, Juliet. More than any of us ever dreamed.

Before Romeo and Juliet, Genesis

There's another epic love story where names also get star billing. It's a love story that trumps Romeo and Juliet in holy spades. It's a story in which our great God is the pro-totypical Actor, making it his mission to redeem the hearts of his creation. It's also a story in which names and the act of naming are also of utmost importance.[2]

In Genesis, God gives man a pretty important task. The Bible says, "The LORD God took the man and put him in the garden of Eden to tend and keep it" (Gen. 2:15 NKJV). The story continues. As God created the animals and the creatures, he "brought them to Adam to see what he would call them. And whatever Adam called each living creature, *that was its name*. So Adam gave names to all the cattle, to the birds of the air, and to every beast of the field" (Gen. 2:19–20 NKJV, italics mine).

Hmmm. I wonder how long that naming session took.

It seems we've been naming things since Eden, and we haven't stopped since. Long before Juliet stood on a balcony asking "What's in a name?," God was already on the scene, showing us the importance of names. Scripture always gets there first.

She Who Must Be Named

I had the once-in-a-lifetime-thrill of being cast in the mid-nineties revival of *Grease* on Broadway, staying with the show for close to two years. To this day, I could perform the hand jive sleepwalking through a blizzard. Almost six hundred and fifty performances will do that to a gal's neural pathways.

I was right out of Carnegie Mellon University—a baby, really—and through an unusual set of God-circumstances was cast in the show. The main roles were being played by folks just a bit older and more experienced than us newbies—stars from TV, film, music, and pop culture—as well as others, and so we younger ones were cast in the ensemble to fill out the show and to step in—or "cover"—when the main characters fell ill or took a vacation. So, in the course of the show, I covered three main characters, or "leads" as they are called, nearly eighty times. And on the other nights, I played my ensemble character.

A character who was nameless, by the way.

At first my ensemble gal—just a tallish, goofy girl—was taking part in the crowd scenes and cafeteria dances. She was a gangly member of the cheerleader squad, oohing and aahing over the cool guys like every other poodle-skirted chick.

But I remember when all that changed. Rehearsals had gone off without a hitch, and next came costume fittings with the famed costume designer. During the fitting, I boldly asked her if I could sport nerdy, horn-rimmed glasses; she thought for a minute (no costume designer makes even the smallest of decisions willy-nilly) and responded in the affirmative.

Within days of working in the glasses, I had it! I finally knew my name! I was Gertrude. And with that name came a flood of a backstory. Gertrude was a newbie. She believed that all the duck-tailed dudes had crushes on her but could not bring themselves to admit it. Though klutzy, Gertie would vie for the head cheerleader spot if she could just get a break. Gertrude was an odd, out-of-bounds character; I'd never played the likes of her.

But because I had a name, I understood my place in the story.

God's Name-Book

All through God's holy story we see the importance of names. Let's take a stroll through some of the most important things names accomplish.

Names Specify

God is the Master of Attention. He can get it any ol' time, any ol' way, any ol' how. Sometimes he employs signs and wonders. Sometimes it's whispers and visions. Sometimes prophets and priests.

But often—quite often—he uses something that seems fairly humdrum. Often, to get someone's undivided attention, God says their name. I've always believed it is so the person would make no mistake about *who* is being called, as well as to communicate intimacy. And though I've never heard God audibly speak my name, I know when he is calling me by name. It stops me midstride and is somehow louder than mere sound. When God calls our names it is as if he is saying, "I mean you and no other." In other words, names specify.

Consider Moses. God called to him from within the bush, "Moses! Moses!" Exodus 3:4 might have sounded like this:

Moses, O Moses, I'm going to send you back to a place where your voice is a hunted voice. But when you say, "Let my people go," kingdoms will rise and fall. Moses, I mean you, and no other.

I'll never forget discovering my favorite, takes-the-cake, say-my-name moment. I was sitting in an open-air Easter Sunday service, almost two decades ago, as my friend and mentor, Pastor Terry Sartain, taught on the power of hearing your name spoken by Jesus. You may know the story. Mary Magdalene has arrived at the tomb, looking for Jesus, whom she has witnessed being brutalized and buried. Wracked by tears, believing someone has stolen his corpse, she pleads with the man standing before her, whom she mistakenly believes to be the gardener, to tell her where his (Jesus's) body is. She is intent on going and getting him. She hears one holy word in response to her query. "Mary!" (John 20:16).

I know all feels lost, but listen. Mary. It is I. Death does not get the final word. Not over me. Not over you. Mary, you will be the first to tell, as you have been the first to see. Mary, I mean you and no other.

Mary, who does not recognize Jesus by sight, recognizes him by *sound* when he says one word: her name.[3] The way he says her name lets her know who is doing the speaking. Stasi Eldredge expresses it exquisitely: "Your name is always safe in Jesus's mouth."[4] The way Jesus says our names lets us know who is doing the speaking.

I frequently meet daughters of God who mistakenly believe that if God were ever to call them by name, he would say it with a dollop of disappointment or dash of disgust. My prayer for you, right now, is that you would believe, even against the clamor of that feeling, that your name will never sound more beautiful than when spoken from the mouth of God. God isn't disappointed in you. Jesus isn't reluctantly picking you for his kickball team because you're the only one left. You're not a leftover to Jesus. You're not an epilogue or an afterthought to God.

When Jesus calls your name specifically, in a very real sense he is saying, "I mean you, daughter, and no other."

Names Identify

In God's grand story, often a person's name will carry with it some sense of a person's identity. The meaning of names gives a sense of the personality/nature of the one being written about. David was indeed beloved. Esau was indeed hairy. Jesus was indeed the One who saves. When we found out we were pregnant with our first son, we settled on the name Levi, because we loved its meaning. Levi means "attached or pledged." We wanted Levi to be "attached" to God all the days of his life, and so we chose a name that reflected that hope about his nature. Our second son's name, Luke, means "light." I can tell you, Luke's personality, like Levi's, reflects his name. He is a redheaded cherry bomb looking for a place to ignite.

We also see this "names = identity" principle in technicolor after God's glory collides head-on with a specific person in a personality-altering encounter. Often the collision is so intense that a name change is necessary. Who that person was before (with an old nature), is not who they are now (with a new nature). Something in identity and temperament has been transformed because of an encounter with a holy God. A new name will be required to contain it.

When you encounter God, the you that goes in is not the you that comes out.

One of my favorite examples of this transformation takes place in Genesis 32. At this point in the story, Jacob is one hot second ahead of trouble. His unruly and hairy bro, Esau, is gaining ground on him. And Jacob is afraid that Esau is coming to exact a pound of flesh for Jacob's dirty dealings years prior. Wisely, Jacob gets his family and traveling farm out of Dodge in order to shield them from the impending blood feud, as he camps out by the river Jabbok.

At some point in the night, the world's most destiny-altering wrestling match commences. Scripture says that an angel/man of the Lord comes to go *mano a mano* with Jacob until daybreak. No referee. No corner water break. No "attaboy" speeches. Just Jacob and a heavenly visitor wrestling out things that needed to be taken to the mat in Jacob's life.

All. Night. Long.

After this epic smackdown, as light is about to break, a wounded Jacob makes an audacious ask of his wrestling partner. "Bless me," Jacob demands. To which the angel/man replies, "What is your name?" (Gen. 32:27). I believe with all my heart that this angel knew Jacob's given name. But there was something mysterious that this heavenly visitor wanted transacted.

You want a blessing? I want a name.

In other words, "Tell me who you are, Jacob: identify yourself. Reveal your reality. Spread your spiritual cards on the table."

In response, Jacob does not throw out a glad handshake or chortle out an introduction, like two buds after a golf game. "Hey, angel. Good to know ya. That was a rough round. I'm Jacob . . ."

Rather, I imagine Jacob bowing painfully, gingerly, his wounded hip aching, his throat raw from the sand, gutting out, "Sir, I am Jacob. I am a heel grasper. I am a master manipulator: I will use whatever I have to, to get whatever I want. I pretended to be someone else. I played a character and lied to steal the blessing from Esau. And, now, rightfully, he is coming for me. That is who I am. I am Jacob."

After that exchange of truth, the angel/man says, "Your name will no longer be Jacob, but Israel, because you have struggled with God and with humans and have overcome" (Gen. 32:28).

Do you see it? Jacob has had an encounter with the messenger of God, and it has changed him to the level of his name. The man that Jacob was when he went in is not the man who comes out. The man who comes out is named

Israel. But he has to give up his old name. That old name is too small to contain the transformation that has occurred by the river. Some biblical thinkers propose that, though Jacob has known his father's God all his life, it is in this experience that Jacob finally knows God as his own God.[5] Everything has changed. "Jacob" fits him no better than old, ill-fitting character shoes.

Israel's new name declares his new nature.

Names Prophesy

Our God is the ultimate Author, knowing the end from the beginning.

Oftentimes, he (or his messengers) would instruct someone to name a child specifically because the name itself would be a sign—a prophecy, if you will. The names predict the truth or future activities of God in and around and through that particular person.

The most famous incidence of this type of prophetic naming is when Jesus's spiritual name is spoken of in Isaiah.

All right then, the Lord himself will give you the sign. Look! The virgin will conceive a child! She will give birth to a son and will call him Immanuel (which means "God is with us"). (Isa. 7:14 NLT)

More than seven hundred years pass before the prophecy is fulfilled in Matthew 1:22–23, "All this took place to fulfill what the Lord had said through the prophet: 'The virgin will conceive and give birth to a son, and they will call him

Immanuel' (which means, 'God with us')." Truly, Jesus was Immanuel, God with us. His spiritual name, spoken seven hundred years before his birth, prophesied who he would be to his people.

Fast-forward to a future prophecy given to encourage those of us who follow Jesus. Interestingly, the overcomers, mentioned in the book of Revelation, have a prophetic name that speaks of a future time: "Hear what the Spirit says, to him who overcomes, I will give some of the hidden manna, and a white stone with a new name written on it known only to him who receives it" (Rev. 2:17, paraphrase).

The overcomers of Revelation will be given a holy nickname, from none other than God himself. Can you even imagine the majesty of those monikers? That near the end of all earthly things God is still naming and renaming his people illustrates the eternal power of a name. From the beginning to the end of God's great narrative, the importance of names shines like a searchlight. And it is one of the very real reasons we have a relentless adversary in this tender area.

An Identity Thief

We got an official-looking IRS letter about twelve months ago. Tending toward the dramatic in this case, I assumed— no, I knew—we were being audited. I just knew it. Visions of IRS agents danced in my head as I imagined us on creaky ladders in the garage, searching for boxes of now moldering deductible receipts. *There goes our Outer Banks trip*, I thought. Reluctantly, I slid my finger underneath the snug seal of the envelope, pulled out the perfectly creased letter, and saw the words—words that I had to read twice to fully comprehend.

It seemed that my husband had been the victim of identity theft. Someone had filed a false EZ tax return in his name, with his social security number, claiming that he was owed a big return from the government. My heart crawled up my throat and sat down. I continued reading, imagining the intractable journey of getting my husband's identity back. I'd heard the horror stories. Thankfully, miraculously, the IRS, knowing our patterns in past years (our taxes are anything but EZ), discovered the ruse. Another boon was that we had recently purchased an identity theft protection plan. If need be, we would have a legal advocate in rightfully securing Jonathan's identity. We would not be left alone in the battle. Yes, there still might have been some hoops to jump through, but in this case the identity thief did not succeed in his efforts to make off with my husband's identity—or his good name.

The application is obvious, isn't it? Many of us live this battle daily. If you have walked with the Christ for any amount of time, you may know that Jesus has given us beautiful, scriptural names—names that set us free into following him wholeheartedly. Names that endow us with holy confidence. Names that enable us to stand in purpose. Names that assure us that we are beloved. Names that shoo off the darkness and escort us into God's glorious light. And we have an enemy who loves to gobble up those beauty-filled names. My friend Penny Blum rightfully calls him the Ultimate Identity Thief.

It's time to evict the thief and take back what he has stolen. It's time to turn on the light.

Sparkler: Have you ever had an encounter with the Ultimate Identity Thief? If so, how has that battle played out in your life? Have you ever considered the power of names in the Bible? What about the power of names and labels in your own life?

5

Spitting Out the Poison

No more will anyone call you Rejected,
   and your country will no more be called
     Ruined.
You'll be called Hephzibah (My Delight),
   and your land Beulah (Married).

                           Isaiah 62:4 MSG

Allison! Wait up!"

I turned to see a venerated comedic actor coming toward me, just as I was about to head up to my dressing room. The sounds of the previous night's pre-Broadway cast party still pinged around my head as he came nearer.

"So, last night, why did you just leave the party without saying anything?"

I yammered something, probably an incoherent mush of apology and excuse, trying at the same time to see if I had particularly offended him in some unknown way. He hadn't thrown the party, or hosted it, but he was a lead in our show and, as such, was a force of personality in our traveling band of actors.

He continued as my face flushed with shame, "It's fine to go, but just don't go without saying anything. Why would you leave and not say good-bye?"

To this day, I don't recall what I said. But I remember what I felt. I felt found out. Like the sheets had been ripped off my life. I'd been leaving events without saying good-bye for as long as I could remember. At least since adolescence. It was just my way, I thought. Slip in. Slip out. No harm. No foul. But my observant cast-mate was the first to put his finger on the pattern and was certainly the first to call it out.

We had been on the road for six months in a pre-Broadway tryout tour for the show. A pre-Broadway tour is where all the kinks are worked out before debuting on the Great White Way. A myriad of scenes had been rechoreographed, reimagined, recostumed. There had been multiple cast parties and events along the way. DC. Boston. Seattle. Detroit. LA.

I wondered how many times my cast-mate had watched me disappear. I wondered what made him finally speak up. I wondered if he knew that it was far easier for me to disappear than to risk feeling like my secret name.

I wondered if somehow, like a psychological savant, he knew I lived and acted my achin' heart out to keep that secret name from floating to the surface of my life, from ever seeing the light of day.

Given Names

My given name is Allison. It means, according to all those baby books that were the rage in the 1970s, "little truthful one." I've long since outgrown the "little" part, but I do hope truthfulness is still a tailor-made fit in my life. I've sure endeavored to live up to my name, and I think about its meaning regularly. How many times in my life have I uttered the words, "Hi, I'm Allison"? Surely, countless thousands. On average, our given names will be the first thing anyone knows about us.

But, for too many years, underneath that innocuous, introductory phrase—*Hi, I'm Allison*—lay a darker reality. A painful half-truth, if you will—a false, character name. It was the name I had given myself around the age of ten; it was a name I had been in a wrestling match with every day since. It kept me running to the shadows. It barred entry to God's light. It kept me careening down halls in search of the closest escape hatch.

My given name may have been Allison, but my more potent name was—*Rejected*.

And though I had never, ever spoken it aloud, its power over my life was undeniable. Unassailable. Like poking an unhealed bruise, my friend had put his finger on that character and that character name I was trapped in.

Typecasting

When an actor is cast in the same type of role over and over again, either because of the appropriateness of their appearance to the role being cast or because of their success in similar roles, it is called typecasting. ("She got rave reviews the last ten times she played the 'girl next door,' so let's make it eleven!") Typecasting is one of the theater's most distasteful bywords. Though it happens *all the time*, it is something dyed-in-the-wool theater folks inherently chafe against, because it means that "type" has triumphed over "talent." For an actor, being repeatedly typecast means playing a type of role you can't escape, even if your talent and training have given you the ability to do so much more.

When typecasting is at work, the good girl is always the good girl. The bad girl? Always the bad girl. Once a sidekick, always the sidekick. It's like the movie *Groundhog Day* for actors. You get stuck playing an unwanted character that you cannot escape.

And typecasting isn't limited to the theater. Sometimes it hops off the stage and into real life.

Often, it is someone else who first typecasts us. "You are this thing, this character, this name." And then, against all reason, we begin to typecast ourselves. *I agree wholeheartedly! I am this thing, this character, this name.* The cycle is an unholy hand in a glove, as we find ourselves playing the same tired character over and over again.

An Unwanted Role

Late grade school leaning toward middle school can be brutal for almost anyone. At that awkward age kids are straining at the boundaries, cobbling together a first sense of identity as well as defining the parameters of what it means to belong, and conversely, what it means *not* to belong. Add to this unstable mix the near-unassailable power of the herd, and the whole environment becomes a minefield—especially if you make the mistake of being different. Or new.

And I was both.

The typecasting started for me in elementary school, when my family relocated from a large southern town to a small one. Obviously, new is difficult at any age. Especially at the ripe old age of ten. One's sea legs take a while to find. I hailed from a large city in another state, where our neighborhoods and schools were not nearly so socially rigid as what I encountered in my new town. Looking back, I believe the typecasting began as I made the mistake of befriending some girls who were outside the normal "herd." And the herd didn't like it. I believe that "mistake," coupled with the fact that I was a different kind of kid—emotional, needy, and artistic—probably did not assist me with fitting in. In the end, it is difficult to identify all the seeds of bullying and mean behavior. I only know that the plant bloomed. Fear found a foothold. The name-calling started. At first, those names were garden variety—silly, even.

But silly mutates into soul-marring. Ugly becomes untrue. And say an untrue thing long enough and it'll start to feel true, especially to a young heart. Those names started sticking to me, emotionally. I didn't know what to do with myself. My little world became unpredictable, mean, insecure. Recess, lunch, and the hallways were often exercises in dread. Sure, I maintained a semblance of normality on the outside (even having some safe friends and places here and there). I "playacted" as if all was well.

In short order, I went from a fairly normalish ten/eleven-year-old with garden-variety insecurities to a shadow girl, chronically absent and desperate to disappear. I remember my mom asking me, one school morning when I was "sick" yet again, if everything was okay at school. She seemed suspicious, but I lied and told her that all was well, acting aggravated at the very suggestion that something was not. I failed to mention being punched in the gut in the elementary hallway by a boy who had become something of a ringleader. I didn't tell her how I had cried in the bathroom, trying to catch my breath, never once thinking of telling my teacher what had happened. I didn't tell her how I steeled myself before going back to class, putting on the best brave act I could muster.

Every day at the beginning of class, I answered "Here" when "Allison" was called, but deep down, I had started to believe I was another name altogether—a secret name I had given to myself to make all the bullying make some sense. And so it began. I agreed with the typecasting. I agreed with the character name.

Rejected.

And even when my family moved to another city in another state, the bullying and *that name* was packed into the moving truck alongside the 1980s white faux-leather sofa.

At first, my new state offered the possibility of a fresh start. I remember willing that it would be so. To assure a clean slate, I tried everything. I would behave like everyone else. (What does that even mean?) I would dress like everyone else. (Hard—I was gangly and uber thin, and I didn't sport the logo-laden attire of the '80s.) I would be the same height as everyone else. (Impossible. Slumping, here we come.) But by then, my false name and the residue of the previous bullying behavior had wormed down into the stuff I was made of and planted a very potent lie, a lie that I now believed. I had ingested the poison. There had to be a fatal flaw, like Aristotle teaches.[1] I was worth rejecting. And so I began the lifelong journey of either

> living and achieving to avoid feeling rejection (proving everyone wrong), or
> living as a rejected person (proving everyone right).

Essentially, my young, astute strategy boiled down to this: be invisible. Invisible people don't get rejected. Never draw anyone's ire or attention. Be smart, but not overly so. Be friendly, but not clingy. Be talented, but no standout. Stay on the edges, but steer clear of the center. Maybe you see why I was always sneaking out of gatherings.

Sometimes the bullying would hibernate for long seasons, giving me the semblance of a normal social life replete with friends and activities, and then it would roar, bearlike, from slumber. Today, I describe it as flip-a-coin living. Heads? Good day, here we come. Tails? Bad day, there we go.

And even when I grew older, and the active bullying ceased, I lived hypervigilant, hyperaware, hyper–on guard. I learned to live a sort of half-life. I became a shadow dweller.

I realize looking back that I simply didn't know how to let someone else in on the pain; I didn't have big enough words for it. Not at that age or at that time. I didn't understand group psychology. I didn't understand the "mean girl/guy" phenomenon. I didn't understand that the enemy of our souls never plays fair. I didn't understand that the age of a target would change his tactics not a whit. I didn't understand that he was (and still is) the ultimate opportunist. There was so much that left me emotionally baffled.

Into this messy, emotional miasma came Jesus, wrapped in the disguise of the theater.

Rise and Shine

I was never an early riser, due to my lifelong battle with insomnia. And this particular Saturday was no different. The dull flip of the light switch was followed by what felt like the dawning of the sun itself, as I rolled my face into the pillow. I was all of fourteen.

"Alli, I'm gonna get a cup of water." I knew what that meant. It meant Mom had already been into my room two or three times—and desperate measures were called for. And though she never poured a glass of cold water over me, the threat never failed to get my big feet on the floor.

I stumbled downstairs to where she had made cheese toast, and started plying myself with cheddary calories. I noticed she had folded the Greensboro *News and Record* into a neat, thin quarter sheet. And something was heavily circled and doodled about (my mother was an inveterate doodler). I suddenly remembered what today was.

"We're going down to the arts center, Alli, remember? The audition? With Livestock Players."

I protested, but this morning my normally go-with-the-flow mother's decision was ironclad. "We're doing it, Alli. We're gonna try."

And we did. I remember being a bit petulant in the red station wagon as we drove downtown, but recall sensing a small bloom of possibility, as well. Arriving at the Arts Center, we went to the second floor, where we signed in and waited to be called to work our magic. More than anything, I remember standing in the middle of a dance studio with rows of folding chairs full of hopefuls who were also waiting their turn.

I inhaled to the bottom of my lungs and belted out a song I had no business singing. The song was about an aging actress who looks back on her life, deeply ruing missed love and opportunities. Not easily accessible emotional fodder for a fourteen-year-old. I was shaky and stared primarily at my feet as I sang lyrics too big for me. I gave it the ol' college try, however, and against the odds, several days later, I was cast. I was in. I would be a part. My first real show was to be *Oklahoma!* (Yes, the exclamation point is an official part of the title.)

I couldn't have known it then, but with some perspective, I realize that Jesus used the theater to begin a process of healing that continues to this day. The theater was the sketch, and the kingdom would be the masterpiece, but I didn't know that yet. I just knew that each time I stood in the back row and sang in the show's finale, I realized I was a part of something. I was a part of a story bigger than myself. My tiny voice mattered. I finally belonged.

And when you know you belong, you can begin to challenge the emotional typecasting. Knowing you belong to something bigger than yourself can wedge a crowbar underneath the boulder of rejection and begin to dislodge it.

Please don't mishear me. This experience wasn't *abracadabra—poof! You're fixed!* On the contrary, it was the beginning of a lengthy work of grace, and though I would still carry around my false name for many years, I finally had a place full of natural experiences that stood in stark contrast to the lie I had swallowed. I finally had a place to challenge emotional typecasting. A place to spit out the poison.

Hindsight being what it is, I'm always amazed at the incredible creativity and relentlessness of Jesus. He will use anything to bring redemption and healing to our hearts, even the back row of a musical or a simple, sticky exercise.

A Truth That Sticks

To me, it was a wild hair of an idea, but about five years ago I started following it, seeing where it might lead.

I stood on the stage of a large Michigan church, asking the women if they would join me in a simple, stark act of bravery. I asked them to write down the false character names they had been born with. I asked them to abandon the typecasting.

The mechanics of the exercise were fairly simple: a blank name tag was left on every chair, and after watching a small, original film I produced with my home church (about the power of false names), the women attending were given the opportunity to fill out the name tags with any false, secret name (or names) that had been plaguing them. Then I asked for them to put their brave pants on, come to the steps of the stage, and exchange the false name for other name tags bearing the beautiful, authentic names God gives to us.

Authentic names like these: Beloved. Accepted. Chosen. Called. Belonging. Justified. Unique. Beautiful. Dearly Loved. Hidden with Christ. Saved. Precious. Prized. Friend of God. Dear. Forgiven. Healed. Redeemed. Apple of the Eye. Anointed. Appointed. Treasured Possession. Head and not the Tail. Capable. Secure. Known. Strong. Salt and Light. Sealed. Conqueror. Sound Mind. Fruit-Bearer. Rooted. Established. God's Poems. All names that offer a powerful, spiritual antidote to the poison that too many of us keep swallowing back.

I jumped into the water first on that Michigan church's stage, explaining that on any given day for most of my life, even at the height of pinnacle experiences like Broadway and Women of Faith—even after walking with Jesus for twenty-plus years—I had until recently believed myself to be Rejected. You could feel some surprise in the room. After all, I was the one standing on the stage, right?

I rolled on, explaining that I lived life trying to either disprove the name or, against all reason, affirm the name. I shared how Jesus wrestled me to the desert floor on that name—no differently than the angel did with Jacob. I told them Jesus had been regularly and repeatedly inviting me to tell the truth on it, to spit it out, like Jacob had done. He assured me that, like Jacob, there was blessing on the other side of doing so. That if I did business with God on this, the *me* that went in wouldn't be the *me* that came out. So I started spitting out the poison.

Sometimes I had to spit *Rejected* out ten times a day, but as I did, I began to apprehend something that I had known for years as a Christ follower but had never truly experienced. I was *accepted*. I was accepted in the Beloved. No translation says it better than the King James: "To the praise of the glory of his grace, wherein he hath made us accepted in the beloved" (Eph. 1:6).

Like the people of God in Isaiah, I would no longer be named Rejected or Ruined. I would be named Delighted In. I would be covenanted to God, and his Son Jesus would never cast me away. If I belonged to no one else, I belonged to Him. (See Isaiah 62:4 and John 6:37.)

No matter what old (or new) circumstance conspired to graffiti my heart with "Rejected," the truth was that in Christ I was accepted. In fact, God had made it so. He had done it out of his own sufficiency. To his own glory. Through his own grace. There was actually nothing I could do about being Accepted. It just *was*, like the horizon. A first kiss. The empty tomb.

My job was simply to agree with grace. Daily. Hourly, if need be. I shared all this from the stage. I shared about living without my character shoes. I revealed my lifelong struggle with my false name, wondering if anyone else had hidden similar false names deep in all those beautiful purses we shouldered into the event.

I also shared with the women that once in prayer, I asked Jesus why living out of a true name—one with evidence of his authorship—was so critical. As I prayed and pondered, he pressed this seed of truth into the soil of my heart: "Allison, you don't call your kids by the wrong proper names, and I don't call mine by the wrong spiritual ones."

I sat down with that for a long time. God doesn't call us by the wrong names.

He never entreats us to come with, "Hey, Stupid! Want to come on a kingdom exploit? Psst! Incapable! Let's go tell the Good News to some folks who have never heard it. Let's roll, Rejected!"

It seems silly and uncomfortable when you see it written out like that, but I know from personal experience and from talking to other women that far too many of us live this way. I surely did.

If we wait for God to call us by our false, inauthentic names, we will be waiting forever. As long as I truly believed I was Rejected, I would never hear him fully when he said, "Accepted Allison, would you follow me into this new thing I have for you? Capable One, would you dare to step where I step, go where I go? Will you allow me to shine through you, Light Bearer? Let's go crack the darkness."

Rejected would bow out of that invitation every time. And if Rejected dared to take a step or two, retreat would quickly follow, because Rejected possessed a hair-trigger, spiritual startle reflex. Rejected always found sophisticated ways to run, if only to avoid the agony of feeling like that name.

But a daughter who knows her true name is Accepted? Now, that girl would check her laces thrice and run headlong at the mountain. That's a grown woman who will step into the light from the shadows.

I shared this with the precious faces that were looking back at me and closed with two words.

Come on.

I said it again. *Come on.*

Let's make the Great Exchange.

False name for true one.

Typecasting for the glorious freedom of the children of God.

Lie for truth.

Shadows for the Light.

And then I waited, wondering if maybe forty or fifty might join in.

After a moment of quiet and no movement, the proverbial floodgate opened and then flung wide. Nearly every woman in the room responded, from the youngest believer to the most mature saint. I chomped a quivering lip as I watched daughters, sisters, mothers, friends, walking up and down the stage until they found that perfect scriptural name and laid down the false ones. Some of them threw the old names, ready to be done with them. Some people crumpled them, ready to forcibly remove them from their lives. Some simply placed them face down, ready to see them no more.

I've since done this exercise for years now. And the stunning thing is that the high level of response never wanes. Usually 80 to 90 percent of any congregation, regardless of denomination, age, racial or socioeconomic background, moves forward to make the Great Exchange.

I've seen everything from Perfect to Prostitute. From Stupid to Stuck. From Invisible to Insane to Ick. From Fat to Forgotten. From Nothing to Nobody. Whore to Horrible. I've seen women put down name tags covered in so many false names that the white space is barely visible. At first I was a little shocked—after all, we all looked pretty put together on the outside—until I remembered my own journey, and how deep the soul-brand of a character name can be. No matter how cute our shoes or white our teeth.

What's in a name, Juliet? What's in a name, daughters of the King?

More than any of us dared to dream.

After the Great Exchange

At one event, after the Great Exchange, most of the women had returned to their seats. All except one, a woman who could have been young enough to be an acting student of mine. The tall, thin girl stood off in a corner; something about her pained expression was familiar. Tears streamed down her face as she clutched a name tag that she couldn't let go of. She was a lot like my falsely-named friend of the previous chapter.

I watched her for a moment and prayed, asking God what I should do. Sometimes a hand on the shoulder is needed, but sometimes a physical hand just adds more weight to a moment God is already fully present in. So, I waited. Actually, people had returned to their seats, and there was a holy hush. The whole company of sisters was waiting, too, willing her to find Jesus's freedom.

Finally, I felt nudged to go to her. As the worship team played on, I went to her and spoke, and she finally opened her hand. On the crumpled name tag was one word: BULLIED. My breath caught sharply, while I reflected on the redemptive symbolism of Jesus. She continued crying as she looked at the names that were still on the stage, waiting to be picked up, waiting to be apprehended. Somehow, I understood that she was having trouble choosing just one. Her pain and her struggle were too big for just one true name. I looked at her and said, "Trust me?" She nodded as I gently turned her around and intentionally covered her entire back in name tags that trumpeted God's truth, whispering them as I did so. I can't explain everything that was happening in that moment—some moments are just pregnant with the activity of God. We have nothing to do with them except showing up for them.

What I can explain is that somehow this girl, who had spent her young life living with the effect of other people's poisonous words, was beginning to leave the shadows for the Light of Jesus. I watched as the Word—the inexhaustible, incomparable Living Word—did battle with all the lies with which she had been labeled. God was rescuing her from spiritual typecasting. He was tearing out the roots of false character names.

A few days later I received a text with a photo of my young friend holding up a notebook which she'd covered with every name I'd placed on her back. And she was smiling. She was shining. Tentatively, but truly.

And I thought, *That's right*. Pick them all. Pick every true name God gives to you and take them with you wherever you go. Remind yourself today. Remind yourself again tomorrow.

As I looked at the image, I shook my head, marveling at how Jesus is still rescuing bullied girls caught in the hallways. How he is always clearing away the mud so that we can find the light we were made for.

As we move into this next chapter, I want to take just a moment to make sure we've all got enough light to navigate with. We've spent some time talking about issues that try to hobble and hurt us—those pesky character shoes and painful character names. Hopefully, you've had a chance to look at your spiritual feet and labels, because once we allow God to encounter us in these areas, we begin moving toward our light in Jesus in greater ways. We begin shining for Christ in ways we never dreamed. Which is exactly what we are going to talk about next.

Sparkler: Have you ever considered the power of living out of a false name? What would it mean for you to sit with Jesus and ask Him to reveal to you what that name is and what His beautiful, authentic name for you really is?

Before the Curtain Rises

An Allegory

> The path of the righteous is like the morn-
> ing sun,
>   shining ever brighter till the full light of
>   day.
>
> Proverbs 4:31

I count my steps.

I keep counting until I reach that door. I've waited for this moment my entire life. I've prepared for it. Fought for it. Sweated for it.

The seed of this one moment has been tucked into every other life-altering moment. And every time I've been the least bit brave or resilient or simply willing, that seed has wriggled closer to the surface. Waiting to break open. Waiting for such a time as this.

A fellow cast-mate swings wide the heavy, metal stage door to the theater and with a tiny bow says, "After you." I look at him and nod my thanks—even if I could find words to speak right now, chances are they'd be lost in the stiff wind.

Entering the theater's backstage area, I carefully write my initials on the sign-in sheet, so the show's stage manager knows I'm in the building. I've never written those two letters more clearly, more thankfully, than on this night.

Because tonight is opening night—and there is only ever one of those.

As I climb the two flights to my dressing room, encouragements trail after me. "Atta girl! Go get 'em! Break a leg!" I smile and say, "Thank you." I've found those two words, at least.

Stopping on the second floor, I pause. There it is: my name in delicate font, taped onto the dressing room's door. This time I open it for myself.

The cool air of the dressing room smells spicy and sweet, like a florist's refrigerated case. Vases sprout from every surface. Roses. Wildflowers. Gerberas. All these floral symbols of support dizzy me. I can't imagine where they have all have come from.

Apart from the carpet of flowers, a twined cluster of Easter lilies stands on a small table—an undying favorite. As I bury my nose in white petals, resurrection's scent rises sharp, lingers long, and reminds me that even dead things can live again. Placing the vase on my dressing table, I slide open the envelope's flap, pulling the simple card from within. I know whose hand has written these words before I ever read them. But still, I need them. These words.

You were made for this.

Nothing more. Nothing else.

Sitting down to the lighted mirror, I whisper those words back to myself, mouthing the phrase like a loop to my racing heart. *You were made for this. You were made for this.*

Over the intercom, the countdown begins.

"Half hour. Half hour to curtain."

And then, in what seems like only seconds: "Fifteen minutes." On goes the microphone, taped up my spine, so that no matter what I do on that stage, I will be heard.

And then the costume, saved until near the end, so that it can remain unwrinkled.

"Ten minutes." My shoes are next. I triple-check the closures, so that no moment will be marred by something as simple as the slip of a shoe.

"Five. We're at five." I turn to the mirror and take everything in, all preparations complete.

And I wait for the final call.

"Places! Places! We're at places for opening night. Again, we are at places." I turn to take a final swig of water as the knock comes. I open the door, already knowing who stands behind it.

"Care if I walk you to your place?" my Director asks.

"Please," I say, looping my arm through his, like old friends. Walking down the stairs toward the stage, I recall every instruction he ever gave. How he believed. How, like a brother, he held up my head when I swore I did not have it in me.

His belief made me believe.

Finally, I arrive at the wings, where my fellow actors will enter and exit the stage all night long. The curtain is closed—the murmur of the crowd and the tuning of the orchestra bleed through it, a muffled symphony.

"It's time," he says, nodding toward the stage and the Grand Story that will be told there.

"I'm afraid."

"Did I choose you for this moment?" To him, fear is nothing but a gnat masquerading as a bird of prey.

"Yes."

"And what else?"

"Whenever you imagine you are alone, imagine again."

"And?" he asks.

"This part of the Story has been given to me to tell, and I must tell it."

"And, finally?" he asks, smiling at what he knows the answer to be.

"Find my light."

"You see that light out there? That's yours. You were made for this."

I take the first step onto the stage.

6

Finding Your Light

There was a time when you were nothing but darkness. Now, as Christians, you are Light itself.

Ephesians 5:8 WNT

*Y*ou could've knocked me over with a sparrow feather. I stood in a crew of students, staring at the cast list and wondering if my high school drama director had committed a colossal typo. I blinked a couple times at what I saw, making sure I didn't need an appointment posthaste with the eye doc.

Slowly, I put my finger on the first character name on the 8 ½ x 11 piece of paper. My finger landed on a character name—Charity. Next, I traced the long ellipsis until my finger rested on my name, Allison. I was all of fifteen, and I had been cast in my first major role. I was to play Charity of

Sweet Charity, one of the theater's most demanding roles. Breathing deeply so I didn't faint, I initialed my acceptance. I felt giddy with possibility and a novel feeling—one that had been growing since my mother's "forced audition"—one of achievement and affirmation. It was new and delicious.

The rehearsal process was dreamy. The alto songs? All in my sweet spot. I even got to smooch a cute senior boy. Cred on the rise! *Sweet Charity* was a once-in-a-lifetime experience. I mean! I was emerging from the shadows. I was going to be in the spotlight, singing Charity's most famous song, "If They Could See Me Now."

Then came tech week.

This is the week (or more) in the theater when all the technical elements of a show are perfected . . . and perfected again. Tech weeks are notoriously laborious, as moments which might take five minutes in the actual show are sometimes worked on for hours—so that they can only take five minutes in the show. The most fine-tuned elements of any show are the lighting cues. From warm washes that light whole scenes to spotlit solos, lighting cues are critically important.

Without them, the audience doesn't know where to turn its attention. The story remains in shadows.

When I stood to sing one of Charity's many solos during tech week, I was to be "picked up" in a spotlight. I was off by a country mile. I had been given a spot in which to stand, but I had blown it. "Stage right. Allison, move three feet stage right," I told myself. I did so, scooching toward my light. When I finally reached my light, my hand instinctively flew up in front of my face. The hot, white light of the spotlight was searing; I saw stars. Suddenly afraid to continue with my blocking and choreography, I feared I might step off the stage altogether, landing Sweet Charity in a full-body cast. Every confident choice from rehearsal became timid and tenuous. Next came the struggle to fully open my eyes under the white-hot light. I remember pancake makeup dripping off my face because my eyes were tearing up. I couldn't see where I was going.

A grueling tech week, to say the least. Ultimately the show would go on successfully and Charity would become a springboard for increased confidence and capacity, but in that moment, as a young and immature actor, I was struggling mightily.

I was struggling to find my light.

Finding Your Light

In theatrical terms, "finding your light" means that the performers sense the exact location of the light (often the brightest spot of the light) onstage, and naturally adjust themselves until they are standing in it.

Performers understand two primary things: they are not responsible to create the light, but they are responsible for finding it. They can't initiate it, but they must inhabit it. Finding your light is a critical skill for any performer, if only because light is critical to the story being told. Light tells the audience where to turn their attention. Light says, "That moment—that moment right there—needs to be seen." Light says, "That moment has weight. All eyes on that moment."

The light assures that the moment will not be missed.

During tech week, calls of "Can you feel the light?" and director notes of "Make sure you find your light" are heard over and over and over. Sometimes a tech run will be stopped as a performer builds in internal cues, helping her find her light, as I had to do with Charity. This is what I was beginning to do, albeit ineffectively, when I played my first lead role at fifteen.

In the theater world, finding your light is a mature actor's skill. A mature actor can sense her light by feel. By experience. She has had so much experience being out of her light, or half in her light, that she knows the difference between that and fully finding it. She knows it is not her job to create the light or control the light, but it is her job to find it, inhabit it, and stand in it as long as she has been directed to do so. She knows she is to bring her fully alive and present self to the light.

A mature actor knows that without proper light, the story remains inscrutable and confusing to those who have come to be moved and changed by the performance. And so, when she is "out of her light," she makes small adjustments until she finds it again. Until she feels that the hottest part of the light (yes, you can feel the heat) is focused right where it is supposed to be. The actor works hard to fully inhabit the illumination so that nothing obscures the story. Being seen, in this case, actually serves something bigger than the actor.

Something way bigger.

At First Light

The house doors open, promptly one half hour before the curtain is to rise on the show everyone has been waiting to see. The crowd rushes in—well-heeled and well-jeaned. The air sizzles with anticipation. The audience knows they are here to witness something special.

You notice that the lights in the house are dimming ever so slightly. This growing darkness is a cue—telling you to settle in, to hush your cell phone, and to peel your eyes for what is to come. Finally the house lights go completely out, to what theater people call "house out" or "house to black."

It's fully dark. But something is coming. You can feel it to your toes. In that short, dark moment—when you can see nothing—actors are positioning themselves, and the show's stage manager is just about to utter some form of the show's most important words. . . .

Lights up!

Suddenly the curtain opens, the darkness shatters; light floods the stage. We can see the epic story begin.

That moment in the theater—from split-second darkness to a glorious flood of light—has always been a living reminder to me of the hair-raising opening of Genesis.

First things first:

In the beginning God created the heavens and the earth. Now the earth was formless and empty, darkness was over the surface of the deep, and the Spirit of God was hovering over the waters. And God said, "Let there be light," and there was light. God saw that the light was good, and he separated the light from the darkness. (Gen. 1:1–5)

These creation-generating words have always sparked intrigue inside me. Not only have I loved the picture of God's

Spirit hovering over the empty darkness (meaning "chaos"), preparing to bring forth something spectacular from it, but I've always wondered: Why those specific first words, Lord? Why not others?

Why are the very first words of God, "Let there be light"?

Now, on the surface, obviously, we needed light and day to exist. We couldn't very well plant and prune, let alone live very long, where we were constantly bumping into one another like bumbling zombies of the apocalypse. Without physical light, life on the whole would be sort of tricky, if not flat-out terrifying. Color us paranoid and vitamin D deficient. Light is critical for just about everything in a natural sense.

But is there something more contained in those words— "let there be light"—than just physical light? This is the God of the universe, after all, whose words create worlds and split ages.

First Words

I have two journals wherein my husband and I have recorded the things our sons have said. The most important entries note our babies' first words. We treasure those words. We remember and rejoice over the slivers of personality they revealed, even at such an early age.

How much more weight should be given to the first words the Maker speaks? Considerable, no doubt. And according to God's first words, light is first. Therefore, light deserves our special attention.

And not just physical light, but spiritual light as well. I believe the physical light of Genesis reflects the spiritual

Light—which is God himself (see 1 John 1:5). That Light will be made known to you and me through his Son, and that Light will shine unashamedly through you and me to a world that is desperate to see it.

There are over 260 references to light—both physical and spiritual—in the New International Version of God's Great Narrative. I want you to take an ultra-quick tour of six passages that give a pretty stunning vista of God's great light. We'll start with one we've already taken a gander at and move forward to the end of the Book.

And God said, "Let there be light," and there was light. (Gen. 1:3)

In him was life, and that life was the light of all mankind. The light shines in the darkness, and the darkness has not overcome it. (John 1:4–5)

You are the light of the world. (Matt. 5:14a)

But if we walk in the light, as he is in the light, we have fellowship with one another. (1 John 1:7a)

For God, who said, "Let light shine out of darkness," made his light shine in our hearts to give us the light of the knowledge of God's glory displayed in the face of Christ. (2 Cor. 4:6)

The city does not need the sun or the moon to shine on it, for the glory of God gives it light, and the Lamb is its lamp. (Rev. 21:23)

From Genesis to Revelation, and every shiny scriptural sparkler in between, the light of God radiates. In creation. In Christ. In the created (us). For the culture.

Since God's Word says we both are a light and have a light in him (see Matt. 5:14 and John 8:12), I want to see us live out this great truth. For us shadow dwellers, it's long past time to agree with Jesus, to strike a match and set it to the wick. It's time to radiate for his glory, to bravely step out onto the God-stages he has ordained for us. It's time to find our light.

Friends, there is no time to waste. In the shadowy days in which we live, God is still concerned with spiritual light. He is ever hovering over the inky waters of chaos and darkness, drawing out light from darkness. And the primary way he is speaking light to anyone still in darkness is through you and me.

Old-School Shiners

There are some old covenant and new covenant "shiners" who light up the God-stage they have been invited to inhabit.

I think first of the Old Testament's Abigail. Abigail is living a normal small-town life when she hears of an egregious gaffe her husband has committed, leaving the people of her small outpost open for a beatdown of the first order. Like a shot, she careens down the open road to convince the young conqueror David to give her people a pass. A "nobody" woman, willing to be noticed (see 1 Sam. 25:23–35). Talk about finding your light.

I think also of Miriam, Moses's sister. At a young age, in an effort to save him from an Egyptian baby-killing decree,

Miriam watches as her baby brother floats down the Nile. When Moses is drawn out by Pharaoh's daughter, Miriam parts the curtain of bulrushes, steps out, and suggests that she knows a wet nurse for the baby. A wet nurse who happens to be their own heartbroken mom. Miriam assures the survival of Israel's great deliverer in that moment. She dares to be visible (see Exod. 2:7).

Abigail and Miriam step out from where they are hidden (small-town enclave, bulrush overgrowth) and dare to step into the light of the story God is telling. And when they step into it, they dare to shine. Each woman is declaring by her actions, "I am willing to be seen that he might be seen." Exposed, even. They are living parables of the Scripture that says, "In the same way, let your light shine before others, so that they may see your good works and give glory to your Father who is in heaven" (Matt. 5:16 ESV).

I'm so convinced that, as women, we need to learn to sense when we are operating in a sphere of God's illumination. When we sense God's whisper saying, "That place right there—I've given you a voice that will carry weight, if you'll dare to use it. I've given you a particular place to be seen because it's the only way they will ever see 'the God who sees'" (see Gen. 16:13).

Friends, this isn't about adding one more thing to the to-do list. In fact, it may be about scratching a great many things off the to-do list—saying no to the good thing, so that a door might open to the "God thing"—so that there is sacred space to listen to the lover of your soul when he says, "That dim place, daughter—I've assigned that place to you. Time to light it up!" A place where our God-infused lives are saying: *This is important. Pay attention. Watch what God is saying here!*

Finding your light on stage is critical for the show. *And finding your light in Christ is critical for the kingdom.*

For so many years, I was the embodiment of these words, sometimes attributed to Plato: "We can easily forgive a child who is afraid of the dark; the real tragedy of life is when men are afraid of the light."

Onstage as in life, I was afraid. I was perhaps the world's most reluctant actor. The same was true of my spiritual scene. I desperately needed my trusted Director to walk me out to my light, that I might sense what it felt like to be in the light as he is in the light. To understand that his light wouldn't burn and expose and shame, but would illuminate and warm and propel me forward into the great tale he is telling. To understand that he had chosen me to stand in specific places to be seen—not for my own glory, but for his. And above all, to understand that he was with me in the light. And that, as is always the case, he had gone first.

The Ultimate Spotlight

The time had finally come.

Angels had announced him. Anna and Simeon had announced him. John the Baptizer had announced him. God the Father had announced him. And now, it was finally time for Jesus to announce himself.

After thirty years of waiting, Jesus returned to Galilee. He returned to his home province, and he took something like an ancient version of a stage—a synagogue, filled with people. Watch him in the following Scriptures, as he returned in the full force of God's Spirit, and stepped into a heavenly spotlight.

And Jesus returned to Galilee in the power of the Spirit, and news about Him spread through all the surrounding district. And He began teaching in their synagogues and was praised by all. And He came to Nazareth, where He had been brought up; and as was His custom, He entered the synagogue on the Sabbath, and stood up to read. And the book of the prophet Isaiah was handed to Him. And He opened the book and found the place where it was written,

"The Spirit of the Lord is upon Me,
Because He anointed Me to preach the gospel to the poor.
He has sent Me to proclaim release to the captives,
And recovery of sight to the blind,
To set free those who are oppressed,
To proclaim the favorable year of the Lord."
And He closed the book, gave it back to the attendant and sat down; and the eyes of all in the synagogue were fixed on Him. And He began to say to them, "Today this Scripture has been fulfilled in your hearing." (Luke 4:14–21 NASB)

With every eye fixed on him, the Light of the World stepped into an appointed place of influence and illumination. As Jesus rose, opening the scroll and declaring himself to be the prophetic fulfillment of Isaiah's words, I wonder if he was already thinking about daughters set free. I wonder if he saw us shedding character shoes and false names and every other thing that dulls us—all in an effort to be free to shine for his glory. I wonder if he saw millions of mothers and mavens and misses stepping into his light, bearing his light, proclaiming his light. Unashamed.

What I know without a shadow of a doubt is that, with every eye on him, the Light of the World stepped into the heavenly spotlight and shined.

What I know without a doubt is that nothing has ever been the same since.

What I know without a doubt is that we have been invited to do the same.

So, let's get down to it.

Sparkler: Have you ever considered that Jesus has a unique place of luminosity for you? Any idea where that might be? Have you ever sensed that moment of being walked out to your light by Jesus himself, and shining there for him? Do you run from or to the light Jesus has given you?

7

Empty Spotlights

But whoever does what is true comes to the light,
so that it may be clearly seen that his works have
been carried out in God.

John 3:21 ESV

Have you ever witnessed an empty spotlight on stage? If you have, you'll never forget it.

Usually an empty spotlight occurs because something extremely unexpected has happened—an actor is backstage popping antacids due to rancid takeout, or a speaker's pant seams have split. No matter the cause, the result is the same: an empty spotlight means that someone or something important is missing. The story freezes, leaving nothing but a solitary, lighted circle. One empty sphere. One empty sphere of influence.

The audience holds its breath, knowing something is dreadfully wrong.

The audience is almost collectively willing the actor to find her light so the story can continue.

Empty Spotlight?

Ever been guilty of the same empty spotlight in your life? I sure have. Especially when I could barely walk due to my character shoes or stand up straight under the weight of my false name. Both had me MIA more times than I care to name. I spent seasons peeking out from the shadows thinking, *I wonder if Jesus has a place that is any less . . . ya know, bright.* A quote sometimes attributed to Abraham Lincoln is, "I am bound to live up to what light I have." During those cloudy years, I did anything but heed honest Abe. Yet as Jesus began to heal me in those areas, my atrophied wings gingerly started to stretch. I began daring to, as John 3:21 says, "come to the light."

As I began winging away, however, I encountered two insidious light-snuffers that interfered with my flight, tempting me to question the whole shining thing. It's time to bring both of those light-snuffers into the light themselves. Maybe you've encountered them a time or two.

One is a decent-sounding lie.

The other? A hard-to-swallow truth.

A Decent-Sounding Lie

The best liars know how to tell a decent-sounding lie. Usually, it's a lie with just enough truth in it so that it sounds believable. At first. Too many times in my own life—especially as it pertains to finding my light in Christ—I've fallen for a particularly decent-sounding lie—hook, line, and sinker.

It's a lie that says: *It doesn't really matter.*

It doesn't really matter if you show up, because anyone else will do in a pinch.

Often feeling and believing that we don't matter—that, on the grand scale of things, it can't possibly matter if we show up to the places of influence God has given us—acts as a convenient escape chute. It lets us off the spiritual hook when things get the least bit challenging. It insulates us from holy risk. It's a line of reasoning that can even sound pseudo-spiritual: *There are so many qualified people, who needs another? I wouldn't want to put my hand to the task when so many people are standing in line. Humility really says I should demure. Wait another year. Or ten. Really, I want others to have a turn in God's light. Really, it doesn't matter. Who am I to think I matter?*

With all the love in the world, may I ask you another question? Who are you to think you don't matter?

Before we go further with this, can we settle a few questions? Should we think of ourselves soberly, as the Scripture says? (See Rom. 12:3.) Without question. Should we consider others better than ourselves? (See Phil. 2:3.) Always. Should we take the seat of least honor? (See Luke 14:10.) Belly up to the kids' table, sister. Should humility reign and ego resign? Yes, ad infinitum.

But I wonder sometimes if some of us are taking Scriptures and scriptural principles like these as licenses to stop stepping up to the life and light God has called us to. I wonder if some of us have even dangerously redefined humility as invisibility.

How many of us think humility is about automatically saying no, when, actually, humility is more about automatically saying yes? Saying yes to God, whatever, whenever, and however. Humility answers in the affirmative.

I remember watching a teacher named James Ryle share on humility, and how God had radically redefined it for him. At the end of his teaching, trying to put the lessons into a mini real-life parable, he stepped out to the center of the stage and said, "If you ask me to put on the crown and rule today my answer is yes. If you ask me to clean toilets tomorrow that answer is yes." *The answer to anything you ask, Jesus, is yes.*

Humility simply says yes, knowing that obedience in all things great and small is the essence of humility, and true humility makes Jesus easier to see. The size of the light isn't the point. The size of our God very much is.

"Will you share your story of recovery, though some eyes may be on you?" Yes. "Will you show up on the board of that struggling ministry?" Yes. "Will you advocate for your son who has autism, though it might ruffle some feathers?" Yes. "Now, daughter, will you move your influence home for a season, as your family needs you?" Yes. "Will you step out of the light, so that another person may take her turn heading the ministry?" Yes. "Will you answer the Bible study question aloud in the group, believing I've actually given you something to say?" Yes. When God issues the invitation, the answer is always yes.

Some things that go without saying still need to be said. So, here goes. The God of the universe can accomplish anything, any way he desires. If he calls us to step upon a God-stage and enter into his light, and we refuse, can he call and equip someone else to do it? No question. Even Mordecai told Esther that if she didn't step into God's light and use her voice for God's people, God himself would find another way: "For if you remain silent at this time, relief and deliverance for the Jews will arise from another place" (Esther 4:14). So, yes, God can raise a cry from someone else's throat. God can call someone else to show up to that heavenly light. God can tap someone else to step into the empty spotlight.

But.

Stay with me, here: Shouldn't there be some spiritual heft to the fact that when he chooses you, it is because he knows there is something about the uniqueness of you—and Christ in you, the hope of glory (Col. 1:27)—that most uniquely suits the glow of the moment at hand? Shouldn't it matter that he wants you on this journey with him as first pick? Shouldn't it matter that he called you by name to a particular God-stage, and not the gal next to you in the pedicure chair?

Surely it matters that you say yes when he calls.

I believe so, and so did my mom.

Mama and the Truth of the Matter

Hearing the word *cancer* is like a blunt-force trauma to the soul, especially when it is said of the one who knew you before you gulped your first breath. Even a decade later, I remember exactly everything. Where I was (corner of the brown sofa). Who spoke the bludgeoning word (my husband).

"Alli, your mom has cancer." His jaw clenched as he went on. "Alli, it's pancreatic. Stage four."

My mom had called Jonathan at work and asked him to deliver the news so I wouldn't have to be alone when I heard. Typical Mom, concerned and pragmatic. Always a step ahead.

That one word—*cancer*—plunged us all into murky waters of grief and desperation. That one word—*cancer*—did its work with deadly precision and unrelenting pace. When the hard-boiled oncology nurse told my brother and me that our mother would be "lucky to get three months," we shook our heads defiantly. Not our mom. Certainly, not my God. And when several months passed, and we bowed to the hard truth—that we would not be getting a miracle on this side of heaven—we put her to bed and tried, with everything in us, to make time crawl.

One night, hoping to inject something transcendent into all the very earthly pain wracking her body, my brother and I put on a VHS tape of one of her favorite singers. She had always been riveted by his every note. In healthier days, I remember the lift in her torso as she would "sing with" his "divine" tones, as she called them. When this man was on stage, a part of Mom was too. This time, though, she was laconic, uninterested. The earthly concert had become background noise as heaven's symphony was growing louder in her ears. My brother had gone off to attend to something in her condo, while I lay with her, still as a stone so as not to move her aching bones.

Halfway through the taped concert, she asked me to turn it down and weakly took my hand. She then turned her head to me and said something I will never forget. (And before I share her words with you, I need you to know I have struggled mightily with whether to share them at all. But I know that from where sweet Patsy Crout sits now, whole and healed in heaven, my mother would want me to share her words with any person reading mine.)

My mother said: "I could have done so much more with my life for Christ."

She paused, her words hanging in midair; I felt shocked. I leapt to defend her against herself. *Mom, no one was more generous. Mom, no one was more self-sacrificing. Mom, no one could have done more. Mom, no. You're wrong.*

She didn't relent in her assessment of her life, and so I just listened, as one listens when eternity hovers. There had been so many places where she had not used her gifts, though she had felt nudged to do so. For a million reasonable reasons, she just hadn't. She seemed to be saying that she felt she had sat on the sidelines on her life with Christ—out of his light—and that she didn't want me to make the same mistake. Through tears, she asked me to make the most of the gifts he had given for the healing of other people. My tears have never trailed so freely. Her words were very hard to hear, but I realized my precious mother was giving me a severe gift. The kind of gift only looming mortality can deliver.

Her gift was an eternal antidote to the decent-sounding lie of "It doesn't matter."

My mother was saying, "Don't ever make the mistake of thinking that it doesn't matter, Alli. Don't ever think that whether you step up to the life Jesus has called you to doesn't matter. It matters."

In the end it may be all that matters.

Frederick Buechner puts it this way: "We must be careful with our lives, for Christ's sake, because it would seem that they are the only lives we are going to have in this puzzling and perilous world, and so they are very precious and what we do with them matters enormously."[1]

Don't let the lie of "it doesn't matter" stop you from taking your light in Jesus.

And don't let a hard-to-swallow truth stop you either.

A Hard-to-Swallow Truth: Too Weak

Dance Guy was an unparalleled dancer and dance teacher. If you possessed a decent double pirouette, study with Dance Guy and you'd have a triumphant triple before you could say "Swan Lake." He was gifted and knew it. His individual attention and expertise could turn you into something special. Someone with the goods to be in the spotlight. With a performing buddy, I miraculously scored a session with Dance Guy. Any opportunity that could transform my gangly self into a real dancer, I was up for. Brain-aching bun and pink tights, here I come.

Dance Guy was charming and intense. And though he made small talk, it was clear that I was being appraised. I suddenly became aware of my hyper-extensive knees, my condor wingspan arms, my general sixteen-year-old klutziness. Dance Guy took us through some deceptively simple combinations so he could see what he was working with.

I remember waiting for our (hopefully) encouraging assessment. He praised my buddy; she was a born dancer! She exhaled, relieved. He turned his eye to me and apologetically said some mash-up of these words: "Allison, I think you are pretty, but far too tall. If you work really, really hard, you might be able to play the lead, where you move your arms beautifully and the real dancers swirl around you. Learn to sing and act, and that could happen. Otherwise, dance-wise, it's the back row."

Dance Guy wasn't mean or cruel, he was just giving me his honest evaluation at the time, and there were things about my dancing deficit that were very accurate. I was young and inexperienced. I was tall. (There is a reason there aren't many world-class, tall female dancers.) There was a wheelbarrow of work to do. But all my young heart took in were his final words, "It's the back row." In other words, you're missing the goods. You're too weak.

Do you ever feel like if you ever dared to step out into the light God has created for you, *your weakness would be the easiest thing to see?*

The Wonder of Weakness

Ironically, the hard reality of my weakness has become a very soft place to fall. When God calls me to stand in his light and I run up against the dirty—*you're too weak*—loop in my head, instead of fighting it, I lean into it. Rather than mount a defense against it, I agree with it, and then I give it to Jesus. Because "you're too weak" actually contains a powerful truth wrapped in emotionally charged verbiage.

In very substantial ways, *I am too weak*, in and of myself.

Sure, I have some natural ability and facility. We all possess some strengths, naturally speaking. But I don't have the career acumen, the emotional resilience, the presence or power to stand in the places he's called me to. Not on my best hair day. Even with all cylinders firing, my natural weakness list is longer than my natural strength list by a country mile. And the same is true on my spiritual scene.

Seriously, if I waited to step into God's light until I had my best self all spit-shined and assured, every weakness heeling like a well-trained dog, I'd be waiting for eternity, plus a day. The same seems to be true for the man who wrote much of the New Testament.

In 2 Corinthians 12:9, the apostle Paul gave his version of the hard-to-swallow truth, as he lived with a thorny weakness that was not going anywhere on this side of the veil. He wrote these upside-down kingdom words, for every weak heart: "But he [Jesus] said to me, 'My grace is sufficient for you, for my power is made perfect in weakness.' Therefore I will boast all the more gladly of my weaknesses, so that the power of Christ may rest upon me" (ESV).

Sit with that beautiful, hard-to-digest truth: God's power is made perfect in our weakness. What an unusual place for God's mighty ability to become whole and complete.

For most of my multiple decades on the terra firma, I've been learning to trot out my strengths, to cradle and curate them, to feature and finesse them above all else. In other words, to bury weakness and to boast in strength. But, as a Jesus chaser, there is an opposite truth. It's a truth that can feel like a bitter spoonful but actually leads to spiritual health, as well as an empowered life. And though weakness itself can never become our identity, I believe God is looking for modern-day Pauls—people who boast. Not just a little, but all the more.

108

In what? In Christ's strength made strong in weakness. Like Paul, who proclaimed, "I'm weak, and contrary to what the world says I should do with that weakness, I'm going to boast in it—all the more—so that the power of Jesus may cover me, weaknesses and all." Jesus uses our strengths—just like he uses every bit of us, but it is in our yielded weakness that God does some of his most empowering work.

When we drop the brave act, leaning into the God who specializes in bringing wonder to weakness, we are certainly finding our light.

A Weak Girl's Prayer

Father, please look on these, my weaknesses. They are many. I bring them, and not my strengths, to you for your consideration. I will not bury this dogged insecurity. I will not bury this fatigue. I will not bury this "I got here by the hair of my chinny chin chin," "perimenopausal mother of a preschooler," "where did I leave my teaching notes" feeling. I will not bury the creeping feeling that all is not well with the world. I will not bury them, but I will boast in them. Look to them and let your strength invade them.

I believe that you make more of my consecrated weaknesses than you do of my so-called strengths. I believe that my weakness is a magnet for your glory. May you make something stunning as the two ignite.

Weakness and Back-Row Glory

Remember Dance Guy's assessment of my dancing ability? Though blunt, his assessment was accurate. Though I would work my twinkle-toes to the nub to become a "real" dancer, it would never happen. I was in Carnegie's "remedial" dance class until my senior year. In fact, by the time I got to Carnegie, I'd had two knee surgeries and a near-devastating ACL tear, making the job all the more challenging.

I soldiered on, the way only youth can. I sensed I was called by the God of the universe to this life, so I worked. I got better, sure. I improved. I sweat like a beast to earn my place on the back row. I became a better dancer during my years at CMU—thanks to some patient teachers—but never a great one. I graduated and was working in Vermont, doing regional Shakespeare, when I got a call from a casting director who had seen me in my senior play at Carnegie. He asked me to come in for a new Broadway production, because they were specifically looking for tall girls. I hustled my bustle to Manhattan.

I remember standing on my first bright-as-all-get-out Broadway stage, singing my vocal cords out, when I heard a disembodied male voice from the dark theater say to me, "Very nice, Allison. Do you have anything more . . . traditional to sing?" I assumed the voice was a producer, and I immediately hopped to, offering a belty, tried-and-true theater classic. I heard the voice say again, "Nice. Thank you."

After being dismissed, I went to the lobby to pack up my character shoes and my leg warmers. The casting director approached me, telling me that the team in the theater didn't feel I was right for the show they were auditioning that day but did think I might be right for another show that was being mounted: a revival of *Grease*.

For hours that night, I got the audition song into my body. The next day, I arrived at the theater, where it was obvious many of the main roles had already been cast. There was a small group of people—far more experienced, far more comfortable in their skin—than I was at twenty-three. Slowly it dawned on me that I was at what is called a "principal call," where they were looking for leads. This was the "bigs" as they say. I took a breath, prayed a prayer, and did my best; I sang, and it was well received. Then came the dance portion, which I knew would be challenging, because *Grease* is known for its athletic, extended dance pieces. I knew where to stand—the back row—where I could hide behind all the other actors, and pray my other skills would be enough.

We went through the paces decently. The steps seemed to fit me. They were plucky and performance-oriented rather than super technical. I was confident in the dance portion of the audition. I thought I made it under the flag. Until. Until they called me out by name and had me dance *alone* with one other dancer on a light-flooded stage. I had seen him dance in the tryouts. He was athletic and sharp, a born dancer. Oh, and he was quite a bit shorter than my six-foot frame. All I could think was, *Great, Mr. Can-Do and Ms. No-Can-Do side by side, doing the steps. Yikes.*

All the other actors parted in a grand semicircle on the stage as I prepared to dance with one other fantastic dancer. Obviously, the production team was trying to see if I could hang with the choreography for real, without being hidden. They were forcibly removing me from the back row. All eyes were on me. The music started and I did my best. I remember praying silently and steeling myself. *This is what you trained for. Ready or not, time to take the stage. Weaknesses and all. God has this, no matter which way it goes.* Miraculously, I didn't miss a step, executing with some style and some sass. However, it was clear as day that, though I could "move really well," I was not, by anyone's definition, a Broadway-level dancer.

And I made it anyway.

Approximately a month later I received a note to call a number with a 212 area code. A woman came on the line and said, "Hi, Allison, we'd like to offer you a role in the Broadway revival of *Grease*." I collapsed on my bed, wondering if they had the right Allison.

When I finally got into rehearsals, months later, one of the music people said to me, "When we were out auditioning for the ensemble, the production team would always remind us when we were casting, 'Now, remember we've already got the tall one from the principal call. Remember the Carnegie girl from New York? She's already cast.'"

I don't want you to miss the way God worked and still works today: my weakness—my lack of dance ability—was actually transformed into a strength by God's great hand and due to his timing. Here's how: when I auditioned for *Grease* at the producer's request, I unknowingly did so at a principal call, where the focus was on acting and singing. At that particular audition my weakness in dancing actually catapulted me into another category—being considered for a principal role. I wonder if they were thinking: *You know, she's not a killer dancer, but she can sing and act. She's young. Could she cover a couple of the leads?* Had I gone to an ensemble call for *Grease*, I likely never would have received that consideration. Due to my lack of dance skill, I would have been cut before I had ever sung a note.

See? In one sense, I didn't have "what it took," but somehow the weakness I was trying so desperately to hide on the back row was transformed into an odd kind of strength. I've seen it in the theater and in real life. I was the gal who always wanted to be invisible, remember? I had grown attached to the back row of the theater, and sometimes of life in general. Until Jesus invaded both, in effect saying, "That weakness you're trying so desperately to hide on the back row—bring that out, lift that high into my light, and watch what happens when my strength is perfected in the weakest place you've got."

I've been compelled—in some small way—to point to the brightness of the One who uses people who wildly boast that they are too weak in and of themselves. The One who uses people who still wildly believe that it matters that they say yes.

Will you, friend? Will you reject the decent-sounding lie that *it doesn't really matter*? And accept the hard-to-swallow truth that, in ourselves, *we are too weak*?

Will you join us as we flutter on toward the light of Christ, trusting the One who is Light itself? By his grace and in his grace, will you "come into the light, that what has been done is done plainly by the power of God"? (John 3:21, paraphrase).

I sure hope so. It's not the same without you.

Sparkler: In the journey toward standing bravely in your light with Jesus, how have you battled those two light-snuffers?

The ones that say "It doesn't matter" and that "you're too weak"? After reading this chapter, how do you feel about them now?

How is God's strength being made perfect right in the place of your very weakness?

8

Finer Points of Light

Quicquid Nitet Notandum—Whatever Shines
Must Be Noted

Royal Astronomical Society motto

Look up at the sky!
Who created all these heavenly lights?
He is the one who leads out their ranks;
he calls them all by name.

Isaiah 40:26 NET

She's passionate about loving kids, and she shines like a human torch when that passion ignites.

I just left her—and three other truly lion-hearted souls—sitting on the steps of our church's stage after concluding a run-through for tomorrow. Tomorrow is when she and a holy trio of ministry leaders will take the stage, presenting the case for why we must become door-openers for the next generation. The team has essentially been given the whole service to present their case. It's a first. As someone who gets to lope alongside such passionate folks, I have watched them pray, plan, and practice for the last month like the lives of our kids depend on it. I've seen their hands and their voices quake with nerves the first time they donned microphones, figuring out how to stand without shifting and deliver the message burning in their hearts. I've seen the fight on the outside, and imagined the assault on the inside. These are people—essential people—who are used to being behind the scenes. They're used to loving differently-abled children and runny-nosed, made-in-the-image-of-God children, but doing it out of the sight of thousands of eyes.

But tomorrow they've been called—I believe, by God himself—to dare to be visible. To take the stage with Jesus and declare his heart. To help us, as the body of Christ, remember that one day we will pass the torch to those soon-to-be leaders, and we want them to firmly grab that torch and thrust it high. We want to tend to the light for those who come next.

As I was packing up from today's rehearsal, the human torch looked at me and said these exact words: "I feel good. I feel ready. But the only thing is, Allison, those lights are bright. I'm not used to it." She looked up to where the lights hung, shielding her eyes.

"You're gonna be great!" I said, smiling. What I thought was: *No getting around it. Those bright lights let your story be seen by the person in the farthest corner of the balcony.*

But man, oh man, when you step into them, are you ever gonna shine.

And shine, they did.

So How Do You Know?

So, at this point, you might be thinking, *Okay, but how do I know? How do I identify God's light for me?* Obviously, we all know we're to radiate and reflect his reputation equally in the grand and in the grind. But how can you identify a set-apart shiny place—a place of influence, risk, and authentic bravery? A lit-up God-stage? Just like Paul knew he was uniquely called to radiate Christ to the Gentile peoples? Or like Gideon knew it was time to step out of the winepress for war? How do you really know, like my friend, who stood upon a God-stage that day under the bright lights?

First, we remind ourselves

1. that it matters;
2. that we are weak in ourselves (but in Christ, our weakness is transformed by perfect strength);
3. that our character shoes can't take us there; and
4. that God calls us by our authentic names, not false ones.

Those attitudes of the heart, mind, and spirit are huge indicators that we have been equipped to stand in a moment of God-ordained light. Those reminders operate like four lodestars in the sky. (Lodestars, by the way, are the "big guns" of navigation by starlight. Think the North Star. Lodestars formed a trusty sky map before compasses revolutionized navigation.)

Though this list is by no means exhaustive, let's look at a few of the "finer points" of light. They might help you spy out God's light for you. They may help you know when to say, "Yes, Jesus, I'm right where I'm supposed to be."

Look Out for What Loosens Your Tongue

I think most of us understand that we need to pay attention to passion when we're trying to identify a place of God's calling and light. But sometimes passion's hallmarks are hard to identify. They can be slippery, as hard to get ahold of as a wet toddler. Hey, they can even be hormonally influenced! (I'm talking from experience. My "passion" to open a bookstore in rural South Carolina might have had its fleeting roots watered by an estrogen flood.) But lasting passion does have a giveaway—and that giveaway is found in our words. Our true heart will always find a way of speaking. Jesus says so (see Matt. 12:34).

I met a wonderful young lady at a conference, and we struck up a conversation. I asked her what she did. She mentioned she worked in the youth department at her church, and she was peppy enough about that. Soon, though, she divulged that she was on the cusp of getting a master's degree in counseling. When I asked her how she planned to use the degree, she said, "I'll counsel, but what I'm really dying to do is to help in the aftercare of women who have been sex-trafficked."

And then it happened, friends. One of those finer points of light. I witnessed her tongue loosen, words flowing like the mighty Mississippi at flood stage. And though she wasn't there yet (we'll talk about waiting in a bit), we both knew that a new light was rising in her sky like a first star of the evening. She positively glowed with passion. She was well on her way to finding God's light for the next season of her life.

Gaze on Your Good Bones

Several years back, I started noticing an interesting phrase as I watched TV. Maybe you did too. Ever watched one of those flippy-floppy house shows and heard the real estate agent say, "This house has good bones"? What are they saying as they praise the skeletal structure of the tiny bungalow perched on a gargantuan bluff? They're saying that no matter what color of mashed-avocado-green paint is on the wall, the house's architecture is sound and stable. The most important things are present; everything else is "just cosmetic." The foundation can be counted on. The house will endure because it has "good bones."

Godly character is the "good bones" of any light you're standing in today, tomorrow, or in the future. And though Jesus is as serious as all-get-out about giving us "good bones" in every area, in my life I have found him to be especially attentive to character development in the area of my calling or, for our purposes here, my light. In fact, without allowing him to build us in the area of our character as it pertains to the spheres of influence he has called us to inhabit, we are in dangerous territory. Any calling minus character is a stick of dynamite with a short, burning fuse. It's a flash grenade about to go boom. Without "good bones," our fickle hearts will often run to boost our own fame rather than bearing the fame of another. Without "good bones" we won't have the structural integrity to hold through the storm.

As someone whose God-given light sometimes involves being in front of people, I can tell you that the Lord has been relentless in my life in the areas of humility, security, and identity. I'm not fully healed yet and won't be until I see him face-to-face, but the work continues, and that is comforting to me. Jesus acts like a spiritual home inspector. He goes beyond the cosmetic to the construction itself. He's always shoring up the foundations, taking a look at the weight-bearing beams, checking for mold—all things that might not cause a problem imminently, but left untended will damage the structure of the house. And though there are times I wish he could take a pause from working in the crawl spaces of my life, I realize that I've got a Master Builder at work doing what he promised—giving me good bones!

Everyone then who hears these words of mine and does them will be like a wise man who built his house on the rock. And the rain fell, and the floods came, and the winds blew and beat on that house, but it did not fall, because it had been founded on the rock. (Matt. 7:24–25 ESV)

Watch Out for the Holy Rub

I think of the "holy rub" like the process of kindling a fire: it's a place where the natural God-gifts of our life rub up against a place of lack or weakness in ourselves. Those two things—our natural God-gifts and weaknesses—rub up against the callings, grace, and empowerment of God. And it is right there in the holy rub that the sparks begin to ignite. And the light of fire cannot be long behind.

Think of Moses and his burning bush.

Moses had natural shepherding and leadership abilities, born of forty years of herding sheep and of his years as a prince of Egypt. Those were Moses's gifts. However, both of those natural gifts rubbed up against a place of profound lack and weakness.

Watch this: when God calls Moses out of the desert shadows into the light of leading God's people to freedom, Moses gives him a litany of personal weakness and lack. To God's invitation Moses says:

Who am I to do this?—What if they do not believe me?—I am slow of tongue and speech.—Please, oh please, send someone else. (Exod. 4:1–13, paraphrase)

But the God who said, "Let there be light!" is undeterred by a little weakness and lack. God persists with Moses, addressing each fragility and flaw with his precious promises, saying, "I'll be with you every step of the way. Let's go, Moses. Time to show up and shine on."

Moses obeys, begins to move with God's plan, and experiences the holy rub—natural gifting, *plus* profound lack, *plus* the grace and ability of God. When Moses follows God, his life moves from the encounter of the burning bush to ultimately leading the people of God by a pillar of night-fire, as he trusts the God of the holy rub.

My Own Holy Rub

I will never forget one of the first times I sat on the porch (where speakers and performers sit) on the Women of Faith tour. We were in Columbus, Ohio, one the ministry's biggest events. I was slated to do a drama—a one-woman drama. Alone. So, imagine it: I was doing a one-woman drama on a stage surrounded on all four sides by . . . women. Thousands and thousands and thousands. Because of my young history, women, as a whole, terrified me. I white-knuckled the sides of my chair and thought, "I can't do this alone." I thought my weakness—that desperate desire to disappear—would overtake any natural acting ability I'd ever been given. But then and there, Jesus lifted me, writing on my heart, "Let's go, Little Truthful One. Everything in your life—your weakness, your wounds, your wonder, has brought you to this place. I am calling you to stand on that stage and speak the truth to hearts that need to hear it. And you are not going alone. I am going with you."

I remember thinking: the I AM is with me, just like he was with Moses. Just like when he called Moses, a tongue-tied mess, to be his mouthpiece.

As I stepped up and took the stage, I could almost feel the mane of the Lion of Judah brushing up against my legs. I was not alone. My mouth flew open to speak and I felt . . . joy. Happiness, even. I felt a sense of "this is it!" This is the unusual joy of the holy rub. Even with all the weakness, it didn't hurt to stand in his light, and it wasn't agony to walk in the moment of his calling. As my brilliant friend Lisa Harper says, "God's calling doesn't necessitate self-flagellation. It will definitely involve working but doesn't have to include wincing!"[1] For me, the battle leading up to taking the God-stage felt brutal, but the doing of it felt beautiful. The experience felt like the best of all worlds—a gift empowered by the Holy Spirit, with a place of need that would always keep me dependent on the grace of Christ himself. All those elements kindled until the spark ignited, reflecting the Source of all true light himself.

Three Shiny Women

I know most of us will never stand on actual theatrical stages, but, as I've said before, I believe *all of us* have a God-stage. A place where we no longer hide. A place where we bring who we are to whose we are, and say, "I'm willing to glow for your glory, Lord."

I want to tell you about three women I know personally who took Jesus's call to shine seriously—wherever and however he was asking them to.

My friend Kandi says these vulnerable words: "I hid on the back row of my church for seven years, frozen in fear. No one really knew. I prayed for release. I prayed for God to help me." Jesus loves "help me" prayers, and began rescuing her from fear's fortress. Over a course of years, Jesus began to invite her to take baby step after baby step, saying, "I've got so much more for you than the shadows, daughter. Will you dare to follow me to the light I have for you?" Kandi did just that—baby step by baby step, following Jesus all the way to working with the kids and the choir, and becoming a megawatt part of church life. She followed Jesus to the light he had for her. She was no longer burying talents; she was digging them up, dusting them off, shining them up.

Heather sang the same song as Kandi, but in a different key. Heather was on track to be one of the youngest-ever vice presidents of a Fortune 500 company. Her position and her pedigree would have been historic at her age. She had everything the world labels "Successful!" The bonuses. The cred. The say-so. And she was doing all this as a rock-solid believer, having unique influence in places not many Christ chasers get to go. After eight years, God started tapping on her heart's door, in effect saying, "Your light is moving home, daughter." Heather answered Jesus's call, though no one much understood it at the time, least of all herself.

Now, after three years of keeping the home fires burning, this is what Heather says of the experience: "The first two years I was home from work are years that I will treasure. They shaped me. God taught me how to rest in his presence and promises. How to hear his heart for his children, how to truly pray for my family. He changed my name from 'corporate' to 'mama' and taught me the deep joy of that new name. I'm still home. There is still a sting, at times, in following God back home. Like Abraham laying Isaac on the altar. That's what it felt like laying down my dreams. Trying desperately to embrace a world of potty training, juice boxes, errands. But the Lord has shown me in the last few years at home that I'm a changed person, and I wouldn't trade all the promotions and recognition in the world for a changed heart."

Kandi left the shadowy back row to light up the body of Christ with her God-given gifts. Heather left the sumptuous light of the boardroom for the night-light of her boy's bedroom. And our third shining star? Well, Cleola took the light of Jesus with her to a dim home, trusting that it would be enough to shatter the darkness into a thousand points of light.

Cleola's Light

In the year of our Lord 2000, when the world had just narrowly escaped plunging off a cliff (Y2K water stockpiles, anybody?)—I discovered a woman who dared to shine. I didn't know just how much until I attended her funeral.

Her name was Cleola Crout.

Cleola had lived her entire life in Pelion—a speck of a town forty miles outside of Columbia, South Carolina. Pelion was an agricultural outpost, where sandy, flat fields of crops dominated the landscape, broken by the occasional house, barn, or trailer. It's the kind of place that, unless you live there or know someone who lives there, you are speeding past down the blacktop.

Cleola's life had never made an obvious splash or provided fodder for anyone's weekly blog, but in heaven's library, I believe the story of her life is tucked alongside the spiritual greats.

I should have known something was up right away because Florence Baptist Church was packed to the gills. Standing room only. This in and of itself is a little unusual for your average eighty-year-old's memorial service. By that age, most elderly folks' funerals are polite affairs, attended by only a smattering of friends and family.

But this homegoing was different. Three pastors offici- ated, three pastors who seemed to forcibly hold themselves back from preaching full sermons about this Cleola woman. Every one of them fought tears as they pressed through their respective eulogies.

The ages of the funeral attendees spanned the generations, from adolescents to those gray and knocking on heaven's door themselves. Genuine emotion moved the congregation. Tears and gentle "amens" bounced around the hull of the small country church for the hour-long service. I heard tell of Miss Cleola's twenty-five years of teaching adult Sunday school; her tireless VBS work; countless meals delivered and people loved; on and on the stories went. She had loved truly and had been truly loved. That was patently, undisputedly clear.

After watching her casket lowered into the church grave- yard, which happened to be right beside the church proper, I was approached by a man in an ill-fitting suit. The man's ankles and wrists were exposed. It seemed as if the polyester specimen he was wearing had been waiting to see the light of day since disco was king. Clearly, the man was trying to do whatever he thought necessary to fit in at Cleola's funeral, but it was obvious he felt like an ultimate outsider.

For some reason—maybe because I had sung at the funeral and that gave him a sense of knowing me—he beelined for me and grabbed my hands. His elderly hands shook as if from alcohol withdrawal. In that moment, I wondered what the story of his life had been. No doubt it had been hard and shaky—just like his hands. He sniffed, gathered his words, leaned in close, and rasped out his secret to me:

Years and years ago, when no one would come to me, when I went through my divorce and my troubles, so many years ago, when no one else would come to me, when no one else would come to see about me, Miss Cleola—Miss Cleola, she came. She sat with me. She brought me a meal. She held my hand. She came to me. Ma'am, your grandmother came to me. I'll never forget that.

And then he dropped my hands and hurried away. I never did get his name.

In decades past, when divorce and addiction stained a person for life, she had gone and held a brokenhearted man's hand. And somehow that one lighthouse moment, that one authentically brave moment, had been a lifeline for a soul so obviously adrift at sea. And no matter how twitchy he felt around churchy things or people, he had come to bear witness to the light of Cleola's life, and how that light had banished his darkness at a kitchen table, if only for a moment.

Standing there in the graveyard of Florence Baptist Church, watching him go, something fell softly into place within me. The hundreds of homegoing attendees. The three pastors. The emotion. The man with the shaking hands. All of it. I understood all of it.

Cleola Crout, my grandmother, had spent her not-so-small life in a very small town, shining. She lived like a magnifying glass, making God easier to see. Without an ounce of fanfare or even much notice until the end, she believed Jesus when he said, "You are the light of the world." She didn't cover her light, she carried it high.

Stretched-Neck Glory

*For all creation, gazing eagerly as if with outstretched neck,
is waiting and longing to see the manifestation of the sons
of God.* (Rom. 8:19 WNT)

All creation is waiting, edge of the seat, neck stretched, to
SEE. The Kandis, the Heathers, the Cleolas, the yous, who
have bravely declared:

> Jesus, if you have ordained that light for me—and given me
> the grace to stand in it—I will do so. Though my feet wobble
> and my voice warbles, though I don't understand, though
> social norms might say "don't," I'll risk being seen, Jesus,
> that you might be easier to see.

*For in the end, it's not the show that matters, it's the show-
ing up.*

Sparkler: Where do you have a holy rub? How is Jesus relentlessly building good bones in a particular area? What loosens
your tongue? In the stories of three shiny women, with whom
do you most identify? One who leaves the shadows, daring
to be visible? One who follows Jesus, leaving large visibility
for a tender place of use? Or, like my grandma, one who was
called to bear the light in secret?

9

Trusting the Director

> [Adam], where are you?
>
> Genesis 3:9

> God takes His stand in the great meeting of His
> people.
>
> Psalm 82:1 NLV

*R*ight now, I am looking at a list of fourteen names.
The list contains the names of fourteen directors—
both of the artistic and spiritual kind—who made the writing
of this book a possibility. Who made me a possibility, in a
way. I wish I could trot out each of their impactful stories
one by one. Lighting room pep talks. Pastors who always
picked up the phone. Insecurity squelchers and confidence

builders. On and on the contribution of good directors goes. Each of them dropped a pebble into the waters of my life, and the concentric circles ripple to this day.

Even if you've never stood on the stage one moment in your life, you have been impacted for good, for ill, or even neutrally, by directors. A director's job description is contained in their very name. Above all, directors provide direction. Anyone who provides direction is, in essence, a type of director. Think "leader." Think "mentor." Think "teacher." Think "boss." Think "cornerman" or "cornerwoman." I'm sure, like me, you've had those key directors and teachers who have shown up in your life at the right time.

Among a million other things, directors provide thoughtful, careful, long-term mapping and strategy. They say, "Look team, this is where we're going." Or, in an actor's case, "This is the way the scene must be played for the story to make sense."

As I look back on my life—in the theater and in the kingdom—great directors have influenced me infinitely. Aside from taking off the character shoes and exchanging my false name for an authentic one, little has assisted me in finding my light more than the beacon-light of good directors. The best ones have lifted me and gently drawn out gifts I didn't know were hiding under the debris of my life. Others have helped me stand in the light God was creating when I would have rather stooped in the shadows. Still others sheltered me with their presence.

As I glance at my Great Directors list, I notice an amazing thing: I trusted them. Every one.

Sunscreen for the Heart

For much of my life, I lived with a sunburned heart in regard to trust.

Whenever there was too much heat, I'd hide. I existed with a trust deficit as deep as the Marianas Trench. Once, a dear friend who happens to be a brilliant Christian counselor looked at me and said, "You might be the most hypervigilant person I know." At first I took it as a compliment. It sounds good, right? Like I'd make a great emotional Navy SEAL, ready for any shadowy threat. But it's no way to live. Trust me. Here's why.

Hypervigilance is often developed when a person cannot trust the way the world will work. It is a way of protecting oneself against any threat—real or perceived. However, as I protected myself from a lot of bad, I also protected myself from a lot of good. It was my way of taking my heart back from God and saying, "I believe I can do a better job of protecting myself than you can." I was saying, "I don't really trust you, Lord."

I needed to learn to trust again. Jesus knew that. And one of the unique ways he began to help me toddle toward trust was by filling my trust deficit with good directors—directors who proved themselves trustworthy. Not perfect—no one is that—but essentially worthy of trust. Ones who were after my good and not my ill. The good directors in my life provided a bit of much needed "spiritual sunscreen" for my sunburned heart. And by degrees the bright sunlight of trusting relationships began to feel a little more familiar than foreign. Like Ava Gardner, I was learning to "trust the director and give him heart and soul."[1]

I'll be honest—I'm still learning, but it's a lesson worth staying with.

If you cannot learn to trust your director, the story you are tasked with telling—onstage and in life—will suffer. If the only view you believe is your own, the view will be narcissistic and small, rather than the other-centered, breath-stealing vista God is offering.

The Good Director

All of us need someone who loves us and truly celebrates us. All of us need someone whose view we trust as much as or even more than our own. Someone who says, "I will dedicate myself to your well-being, even when you don't understand." Who looks at us on our worst day and sees our best days still ahead.

How do you recognize a good director or leader in your life? Following are two simple attributes the best directors (artistic and otherwise) in my life have had in common. And, though by no means exhaustive or exclusive, these two attributes are a quick way of identifying a potentially good director in your life.

They ask something of you.

They give something to you.

The Asking

I was a tall, gawky teenager with a flair for the dramatic and big hopes to carve out a career in the theater. The time had come to begin the round of college applications; heave-ho-ing huge college catalogs that were coming to our small condo mailbox had become each afternoon's ritual. I remember Dan Seaman, whom everyone in the theater called Sea for short, pulling me aside one afternoon after rehearsal. On the Weaver Center stage in Greensboro, North Carolina, under the hot PAR can lights, he asked me one question: "Allison, where do you want to go for college?"

For some reason, I immediately responded with a question of my own. "Where do *you* think I should go for college, Sea?"

He paused and nodded slightly. *Uh-oh. Not good*, I thought. Sea was notoriously honest. Not brutally so, just notoriously so. You didn't become the director of one of the country's most highly decorated magnet arts programs, Ensemble Theatre Company, without a healthy dose of judicious appraisal. I braced myself, surmising that I already knew exactly what Sea was going to say. I imagined a word bubble over Sea's head: "Allison, I think Chapel Hill would be your best bet." I would have had to utilize every acting skill in the book not to let my disappointment show if that had been his answer.

Now, just in case there are any Tar Heel fans or alumni reading, let me say, the University of North Carolina at Chapel Hill is a fabulous school, and in my Carolina world, almost everyone I knew was gunning to be a Tar Heel from the womb. UNC–CH is a doozy to get into, and regularly turns out leaders in every field. But I wanted to be an actor, and at that time Chapel Hill wasn't known as a top theater school. If Sea had said, "Chapel Hill," that meant that as much as he loved me, he didn't think I had the gift set to make a real go of a life in the theater. I waited for his answer and found I was in for a God-sized surprise—a God-ordained answer to a question. Sea said three letters that would change the course of my life forever. "CMU."

"Come again?" I'm sure my face said it, if not my actual mouth.

"CMU, Allison. Carnegie Mellon University in Pittsburgh." He went on to explain that those who make it in the theater have to have a tricky mix of responsibility and acumen and gifting. And amazingly, Sea thought I had it!

I was gobsmacked. At that time, getting into Carnegie's theater conservatory took a near miracle. The chances of getting in were beyond steep—especially for a woman. But because Sea believed in me—and I knew that his belief was not a cheap commodity—I believed too. I trusted my director's view of things more than mine, enough to apply for early decision. Waiting to audition for CMU in the hall with all the obvious mega-talents from around the country, I said to myself, *One of these things is not like the others.* What buoyed me in those terrifying moments was that Sea thought I could do it. He saw something in me I did not yet see in myself. Five months later an acceptance letter arrived; I would be a Carnegie Mellon acting student. And by the time I walked for my diploma, I would be a young woman forever ruined for the ordinary by Christ himself.

Please don't miss the simple, initial tool that the Lord used to get my life on his perfect path. That tool *was a question.*

"Allison, where do you want to go for college?"

I have spent many hours wondering about the trajectory of my life had Sea never asked me that simple question. I believe I would've gone to school where I was expected to go to school. In my wildest heart I never would have dreamed of something as box-busting as Carnegie.

It wasn't until recently that I noticed another word hidden in the word *question*. *Quest*ion. How perfect! Well-placed questions can set us on the quest of a lifetime. And can even change our lives forever:

Do you want to get married? Will you forgive me? Would you like to know this Jesus?

I am standing here all because of a great director and a great question. I am standing here because something was asked of me.

Ask or Bust

It might surprise you to know how many of the best directors go about their work.

Let's say that rehearsal is close to complete. The scene has wrapped. The actor has taken a different tack on the character. It's risky. It's bold. But it's not quite working. Often, rather than a prescriptive approach—"Allison, that's not working and here's what to change"—you might hear the director apply what I call an inquisitive approach. "Allison, would you tell me what you were thinking as you approached that scene today?"

The director is trying to get to motivation, to uncover the "why" of the choices the actor is making. And a question is the most exact tool with which to do that. Questions say, "I'm interested in your thoughts and feelings." A good director is not interested in a human puppet that simply executes as told. That would be caricature. Acting is far more than limps and accents and costumes, obviously. A good director wants the choices to come from a truthful place in the actor, from something the actor knows intimately and honestly. Good acting is essentially an internal reality, not an outward "show." A good director wants the why of what you do. He wants to understand your motivation. And the best way to get to that is to ask.

The best directors I have ever had have been deeply fond of questions.

The Prototypical Director

There was another great director, the greatest Director who has ever lived—a Director named Jesus, whom many called Rabbi, who also had a fondness for asking life-altering questions. You might be surprised to find out just how many. Certain translations contain as many as one hundred questions that Jesus asked.

For instance:

Who do you say that I am? * Woman, will you give me a drink?
Why are you so afraid? * Do you believe I am able to do this?
Are you able to drink the cup I am to drink? * Do you love me?
Do you want to go away as well? * Do you want to be healed?

Woman, why are you crying? Who is it you are looking for?[2]

I always reflect on the fact that the One asking already knew the answer to every single question proceeding out of his mouth. He knew all, and yet he still *asked*. Why would he ask if he already knew the answer?

Could it be for these audacious reasons: That Jesus wants to show his deep engagement with and care for those he created? That he is interested in how we think and feel and process? And perhaps most life-altering: That he wants *us* to know the contents of our hearts the way that he already does?

The First Question

The first question of the Bible has always flat-ironed my frizzy hair. When I was a young believer, I thought the whole scene to be a cosmic hide-and-seek. Adam has eaten the forbidden fruit, has taken the first deep dive into shame and hiding, and God has come to walk and talk with Adam as he always does in the garden. Except Adam has blown off the daily engagement, so God asks, "Adam, where are you?"

Sit with that for just a second. Just a simple, innocuous question. "Where are you?"

Do we really think the eternal God doesn't know where Adam is? Do we think he doesn't see him hiding behind the particularly beefy fig tree? No, of course not. Who doesn't know where Adam is? Adam. Adam doesn't know where Adam is.

And I believe that when Adam dares to answer the very first question from God—"Where are you?"—Adam finally knows where he is. Not geographically, but spiritually, emotionally, relationally. Sometimes answering a God-question can tell us where we really are, in the ways that actually matter.

To God's questions Adam answers: "I am naked and afraid. I blame the woman you gave me. I have been deceived."

Adam, where are you? Sister, where are you? Where are you, really? The God of the universe cares enough to know. And when you dare to answer his questions, your own heart will be revealed to you. And then the work can begin.

Looking for a good director? One who helps you take the first shaky steps toward finding your light or who can be a source of encouragement if you are already there? Find someone who is interested; find someone who is inquisitive; find a good question asker. That person will lead you to the *why* of the truth, and that's a truth that can be trusted. Directors who ask something of you are worth their weight in truffle-oil dark chocolate. When you find one, listen and answer well.

Remember, though, not only do good directors ask something of you, they give something to you as well.

The Director's Gift

One of my favorite collegiate classes was called "Styles." Taught by a brilliant woman, the course concerned all the mannerisms and mores that we as moderns were unfamiliar with, but that as actors, we needed to know, especially when cast in classical pieces like Shakespeare or Molière. Women needed to know the vagaries of conversing with a fan. (People, the fan was the emoji of centuries past!) Men needed to know how to comport themselves in public when women were present, especially when a lady entered the room. Think Victorian-era dinner scenes. As a woman enters the room, the men cease their conversations, push back their chairs, and stand. Always. There is something about standing that demonstrates courtesy, obviously, but there is something more to it. Standing for another says, "I acknowledge your presence. You matter. I see you there."

A Great Gift

I cannot count the times I have witnessed my directors standing at the back of the theater for the duration of the show. Hundreds of times. Over the darkened theater packed to the gills with attendees, I can still see the silhouettes of some of my earliest directors standing sentinel at the back railing of the Carolina Theater, as I first learned how to take my light on the large and intimidating stage. Even if I was nervous in a choice or a song or a moment, as I looked out over the house, I could see them like shadowy lighthouses on the horizon. They stood for me. They stood for all of us.

Their standing posture said, "As long as you are on that stage, I will stand by." Even now, due to the example of my earliest directors, I usually stand in the tech booth for the duration of any show I have the honor of directing or codirecting. For directors, standing (if physically possible, obviously) runs in our blood. I believe it is why, innately, you might see a whole arena stand as the final shot is being thrown into the basket or why many of us stand during worship. The book of Nehemiah says that when Ezra the scribe brought out the law of Moses, the people took a stand as "one man" as he began to read the solemn words (Nehemiah 8 ESV).

Something in us knows that when we stand together we are partakers of the same moment.

The Secret Stander

I had the great joy of appearing with Women of Faith for three years, doing one-woman dramas at their events. I regularly pinched myself because of the thrill and honor of being among such gleaming speakers and authors. Truly God delights in using the foolish things of the world to confound the wise (1 Cor. 1:27)!

My final year with them, I had been asked to write my own one-woman pieces, and I was tickled crimson to do so. And more than a smidge intimidated. One comedic piece was a complex parody about a woman's nightmare of being on a dance show, where she was constantly criticized and judged. The piece was a sanctified three-ring circus. There was wacky choreography, multiple video elements (where I played all three judges), as well as the character onstage, voice-overs, and music.

Before the first event, the time had come to "tech" the piece in the arena. All the artistic and head staff had already gone back to the hotel. It was just the tech team and me. So a-teching we went. (Remember, this is where we iron out every technical wrinkle.) To be blunt, it was a doozy of a process. Complex, time-consuming. Stop and start. Start and stop. Stop. The tech team, as ever, was top-drawer. Never a frayed edge among any of them.

But not so with me. Inside I was unraveling at the seams. As we continued, I started to feel more and more spun. Insecurity was whirling me around the dance floor. I couldn't get a handle on the piece I had written. I questioned everything. *Was it stupid? Too much? Remotely funny? Should've hired someone else to write this thing. Should've hired someone else to act this thing.*

Despite the difficulty, I soldiered on, honoring the tech team's time, but inside I was going dark. Finally, the tech team was satisfied that they had it, and the whole internal ordeal was over. I don't think anyone in the arena was the wiser.

I said my thank-yous, grabbed my bags, and started the long walk down the arena's pitch-black aisle past thousands of empty seats. I glanced up to make sure I was headed to the correct exit for the shuttle. To my shock, at the end of the aisle was a silhouette. A petite, feminine silhouette with a purse perched on the ledge beside her. Whoever it was, she was standing. Waiting. Watching. I blinked, wondering who in the world it could be, who it was that was standing there, just like any of the best directors I had ever had way back at the Carolina Theater.

I continued walking, blinking back tears. The silhouette's face broke open into a vivid smile. I knew that smile, that face, that beautiful white hair. It was none other than one of the core speakers, Marilyn Meberg. I don't know if I managed any words, but she read the shoulder-shruggy gesture that said, *What in the world?*—and Marilyn took it from there, saying some semblance of these words: "We were all going back to the hotel on the shuttle, and I just felt nudged to come back and wait for you. The drama is going to be perfect, Allison. Want to grab dinner?"

She'd been there the whole time. She'd been standing by, like a good director. I had not been alone. I had not been directorless. Someone was standing for me, though I didn't have an inkling. To this day, it is one of the most loving things anyone has ever done for me. And it is one of the things that looks the most like Jesus.

Someone stands for you too, friend—even as you do the work to occupy the light he has given. Even if you do not feel it, your Good Director is there. He is always asking something life-giving of you and is always giving something to you. He is always standing by.

Your Director's name is Jesus, and you can trust him.

Sparkler: Think of a "good director" from your life—perhaps a teacher, family member, neighbor, or friend. How did they influence your life for good? What did you learn from them? Do you believe that Jesus is always standing by, even when you cannot see him?

10

You Are
What You Rehearse

I have hidden your word in my heart,
that I might not sin against you.

Psalm 119:11 NLT

*W*hen I was in the Broadway revival of *Grease*, I was
often called upon to perform the leading roles of
Marty, Patty Simcox, and Ms. Lynch with little to no warning.
In fact, I performed these roles numerous times in my tenure
with the show. Once the show opened, it was my responsibility to *stay* rehearsed, especially since formal rehearsals
had ceased. I carried around a four-inch-thick notebook at
all times, and many nights I stood in the wings and marked
(went through) all of my characters' choreography. Carrying

three roles (plus the one I performed regularly) around in your head required a truckload of rehearsal. And when I got the call that I was on in a particular role, I came in an hour before everyone else to an empty theater and "rehearsed" my show in the dim work lights.

Rehearsal stems from an archaic French word that means "to repeat."[1] In a very real sense, actors are what they repeat. What they do over and over again. What they rehearse. What they hide inside.

As believers, we are also what we rehearse—and what we repeat day after day. There is undeniable potency in holy repetition, and I for one have deep need for it. If we rehearse the truth that we are indeed the beloved of God, then when circumstances challenge that immutable truth, like an actor, muscle memory will take over. The truth will rise. The lie will sink.

What we have rehearsed on our best days will be true on our worst.

And what we have rehearsed in the dark will be true in the light.

Holy Hook

Psalm 136 is one of those psalms that has always piqued my interest. Sometimes called the "Great Hallel," or the "Great Praise," Psalm 136 is a lengthy walk through the halls of the history of God's people. From Creation to captivity, and from Egypt escape to eating honey in a land of promise, it's a sung documentary of the life of the people of God, with God's faithfulness as the main refrain. But as much as I am intrigued by its content, it is the construction of Psalm 136 that makes me lean in. Because after each and every phrase, four words are repeated. Like a modern-day musical hook.

His love endures forever.

Here's just a snippet of Psalm 136 in action (vv. 1–4).

> Give thanks to the LORD, for he is good.
>   *His love endures forever.*
> Give thanks to the God of gods.
>   *His love endures forever.*
> Give thanks to the Lord of lords:
>   *His love endures forever.*
> To him who alone does great wonders,
>   *His love endures forever.*

This beautiful call and response goes on for twenty-two more verses. All in all, that phrase, "His love endures forever," is repeated a total of twenty-six times! The author has got that ditty on loop.

It is interesting to note that the Bible records the singing of this same phrase in three places other than the book of Psalms. The first occurrence is in 2 Chronicles 5, at the consecration of God's temple. Here, the Bible notes that the large cast of priests, singers, and trumpeters repeat "His love endures forever" and God blows the spiritual doors off the place. People are flattened like pancakes in his presence.

The second appearance of the holy hook occurs later in 2 Chronicles, under very different circumstances. Rather than a song of blessing, the phrase is transformed into a battle hymn. Second Chronicles 20 records that the singers have been instructed by King Jehoshaphat to go *in front* of the army as they march down into the desert of Tekoa against their enemies. I bet you can guess the phrase in their mouths. Verse 21 records this truth: "As they [the singers] went out at the head of the army, saying: 'Give thanks to the LORD, for his love endures forever.'" God swats away the enemy like they are demonic mosquitoes.

The third, and perhaps my favorite appearance, is in the book of Ezra, when the temple is rebuilt after lying in ruins for almost a century. At the reconsecration, we find the Levites singing a song with the prominent hook.

And the psalm whose ever-looping chorus is "His love endures forever" was perfect for all three events. A beginning. A battle. A rebuilding. His enduring love is the dominant note.

In many ways, the nation of Israel must've known that they themselves were the songs they sang. And so, at the most momentous occasions of national life, they chose carefully what they would repeat.

We are the songs we sing too. Especially the songs we repeat. When we repeat holy things, when we rehearse the truth, it becomes an enduring part of us. The opposite is also true. When we rehearse the lie, it becomes an enduring part of us. It has me asking: *What's on repeat in my life? What am I rehearsing?*

People of the Book

People of Jewish descent are often called "people of the Book." Christ followers could also be called, in a very real way, people of the Book. And, in a different way, so are actors.

For example, the dialogue in a musical is part of the libretto—however, in actor-speak, the dialogue is often referred to as "the book." In a play without music, the entire script is often called "the book."

On and Off

Let's say you've just been cast in a new show and your rehearsal schedule has dinged its way into your inbox. Aside from the where and when logistics, there will come a day that any experienced actor will be looking for, simply called, in actor-speak, "off-book." Usually several weeks before tech week, the off-book deadline is the day when the scripts—which contain the words you are tasked with embodying—must be placed to the side. The words you have repeated, you must now know. The words you carried in your hands must now be in mind and heart. What you have practiced must become a part of you. That's what being "off-book" means to an actor.

But before you get to that semi-nerve-wracking "off-book" day, you walk through rehearsals "on-book." Have you seen videos of actors rehearsing with a pencil in one hand and a dangling script in the other? Perhaps you've seen photos of a play's first rehearsal with the performers doing a "read-through." Every actor's primary focus will be on the script, the book, because it tells them what to do and say. It gives them the arc of the story, the motivation of the characters, as well the blazing heart of the playwright. The first rehearsal starts "on-book," and the whole rehearsal process is held together by respect for the book. One of the most

147

time-honored relationships in the theater is the one between the author and the actor. We never want to misspeak or misuse the words of the author. We honor the words on the page, and are taught early that this honor is the cornerstone for every actor's work:

Trust the written words. Trust the book. Trust what you have rehearsed.

The Book is Boss.

For believers, God's Book is boss too. The same care and concentration that actors and directors express for the script should mark our lives for God's Great Book. I think of the great Scripture, "I have hidden your word in my heart that I might not sin against you" (Psalm 119:11) as a holy cry to the power of working God's Book deeply within—so deeply that when challenge comes, the truth that has been worked *in* will be worked *out*. What has been rehearsed will rise. What has been repeated will reign. What has been practiced will prevail.

I have to remind myself constantly: When in a tough spot, return to the Book. When lost in the story, return to the Book. When unsure of the next right move, return to the Book. Without it, I am untethered, adrift from the larger story.

And the larger story is where life and God's light ultimately exist.

My Ugly Book

Just yesterday I was hunting for something for this book, and I went to the shelves that contain all my old scripts. It's been quite a while since I had reason to open those cabinets, but when I did, it was like opening up a short history of myself. In a moment of reverie, I opened a few of the scripts and marveled. Many of the lines were still a part of me, somewhere deep within. Some of them I still knew by heart.

I've held many great scripts and books in my hands and have had the honor of playing many iconic roles in the theater. But there is no book, no script, if you will, so precious to me as my Ugly Book.

I've got a confession to make: I have a DTV. Where the spine and cover of my Bible used to be, there are five pieces of that universal fixer of all things—duct tape. Maybe you have a Bible that proudly displays NIV, KJV, ESV, or NKJV on the cover. Me? I've got a DTV. My Duct-Taped Version and I have traveled more than a few miles together.

The initial damage to my Bible occurred when I moved from Pittsburgh to New York after college. An entire bottle of nail polish remover had somehow wriggled free on the floor of my secondhand Supra, spilling all of its contents onto said Scripture. I can remember shrieking as I unpacked that blessed Book, realizing the remover had left a pungent smell, along with a telltale water mark on every page, and had already begun the work of eating through the spine and binding. I was devastated in a way that only a twenty-three-year-old actor can be, which is to say, dramatically.

You see, I had been the quintessential prodigal who had come to herself and come to the Lover of her soul during her college tenure. When the spiritual light switched on for me, that Bible—the one now soaked in nail polish remover—had been a beacon. I scrawled notes, scribbled secret prayers, highlighted, underlined, dog-eared, cried over, spilled on, and pored over that Book by an Author who was saving me from me.

Now it was ruined, and it smelled funny to boot. But I simply couldn't abandon it. Those who loved me attempted an intervention. Graduation, birthday, and Christmas presents became predictable: Bibles—shiny and new. One was even painted by a gifted artist. I saw behind their subterfuge: my friends were embarrassed by the state of my Bible. I graciously accepted their gifts, slapped some duct tape on ol' faithful, and kept trucking.

Once, many years later, my husband, Jonathan (Tall Man), bought me a tastefully-crafted leather cover for my dilapidated Bible, but by that time, anything so pristine felt foreign in my hands. I had come to appreciate the tattered feel of the DTV.

On a deeper level, I suspect that my Bible's rough-and-tumble appearance was a memorial of sorts—a visceral reminder of how God takes the shards of a broken life and creates something useful and good. When I let go of counterfeit affection, that Book exhorted me: "Return to me" (Is. 44:22). When I married a man far more good (and good-looking) than I ever could have dared dream, that Book said to me, "Eye has not seen, nor ear heard, nor have entered into the heart of man the things which God has prepared for those who love Him" (1 Cor. 2:9 NKJV). When I buried my beloved mother, that Bible said, "Precious in the sight of the LORD is the death of his saints" (Ps. 116:15 KJV). When my son was born, that Bible said, "I will boast all the more gladly about my weaknesses, so that Christ's power may rest on me" (2 Cor. 12:9). When my second son was born when I was forty-one, after months of bed rest, the Book again said, "Boast all *the more gladly* in your weakness that the power of Christ may rest upon you."

The pieces of duct tape are still there, holding together the topography of my redemption. It strikes me that in so many ways we are all a little like my duct-taped Bible. Frayed around the edges, marked by beauty and desperation, often in equal measures, and held together by a God—and a Book—who never lets go.

Reverence

Aside from rehearsing the words of God's Great Book regularly, there is another practice—gratitude—that I also have to rehearse daily, lest my shine grow dull.

There is a tradition at the end of many ballet classes that I find humbling and comforting, called "reverence." It's a danced movement that takes its name from a French word meaning "to revere," often by bowing or curtseying. Reverence is a short choreographed moment when, through a beautiful series of curtseys, bows, and arm movements, the class thanks the teacher for the class and the accompanist for the music.

Thank you for the lesson. Thank you for the music.

Reverence is a beautiful way of marking the moment with gratitude, of saying, no matter how grueling or grand the lesson, "I thank you for it. I honor you for your investment in us as students." In some of my collegiate classes my teacher performed the reverence in kind, thanking us for being willing students.

Reverence was never to be missed; it was repeated at the end of every ballet class. Without fail. Each curtsey said, "I revere you, and I acknowledge this lesson—hard or heavenly." Every unfurled arm whispered, "I honor your wisdom, your tutelage." Reverence, in essence, is a liturgy of movement, a bodily way of "giving honor to whom honor is due" (Rom. 13:7, paraphrase).

I've done the reverence with buckling knees, sapped from the demands of class. I've done the reverence with a withering heart because the class moved to another skill that was beyond me. I've done it with delight, mastering that same skill after months of repeating it. I've even done the reverence teary-eyed, as the time had come to move on to another class or grade or city. In whatever state I found myself, I rehearsed the reverence. I repeated it. We all did.

We were just who we were, saying "thank you" with all we were.

I Will Be What I Have Rehearsed

Friends, I know from firsthand experience that when I am in a dry and dark place, it is my love of the Book and my reverence that will be assaulted first. In those places, I'm so lured to go "off-book" and write my own story. I'm tempted to flirt with the *drama* of ingratitude rather than fling myself upon the God who invites me to dance, saying, "Thank you for the lesson."

After three decades of walking with Jesus, I have come to discover that I have to return to the holy repetition of both of these things. The Book leads me to his light and keeps me from chasing counterfeit "lights." And rehearsing gratitude? Well, gratitude allows me to stand in his light winsomely and humbly. Gratitude allows me to remember whose grace first struck the match.

For even when a desert season descends and my plans come to naught, or the call comes that I dread, I know now that what has been repeated will be the first thing to rise.

I will be what I have rehearsed.

Sparkler: Friend, what are you rehearsing and repeating in your life? Do you believe that you will be what you have rehearsed? How so? How are the Book and the reverence a part of that rehearsal?

11

Waiting in the Wings

Because you are my helper,
  I sing for joy in the shadow of your
  wings.

Psalm 63:7 NLT

When I entered my young adult years, I galloped through much of life like a clumsy filly. I had a deeply ingrained habit of running ahead of God, audaciously asking him to catch up. (The arrogance!) I was always on the move, always on the cusp of some "great" endeavor or another. Some of that tendency, no doubt, was due to immaturity and a tendency to run on emotional fuel. But some of it was deep, dyed-in-the-wool impatience. I craved the "now" of God but chafed against the "not yet" of God. I recall the internal cringe when someone would pray for me to "surrender to the waiting, knowing that those who wait upon the Lord renew their strength and mount up with wings like eagles" (see Isa. 40:31). Although I certainly wanted to soar like an eagle, I didn't want the "wait" that preceded it. Naïvely, I equated waiting time with wasted time. I equated waiting with nothingness.

What I didn't realize was that I was being invited into the part of the story that cannot be minimized, skipped, or sped up. It was the place in the capital *D* Drama that all of us must learn to befriend, as we will visit it over and over again. It is the place that the Father of lights ordains and inhabits that will prepare us fully to find and stand in any light he has provided.

It is a place called "the wings." And it is where the waiting is done.

The Wings

For a performer, the wings of a theater (that part of a stage that is out of sight of the audience, typically marked with tall fabric, called "legs") are a place of coverage and preparation, all in one. The wings are bustling with activity, just out of sight. In the wings, necessities are being attended to. Costume changes are being prepped. The dancer with the oddly swollen ankle is donning an ice bag. The nervous soloist is singing his first line under his breath. Another actor is praying before the entrance.

To the actor, the wings are a holy space. Revered. Chitchat is usually nonexistent—especially during a performance. Shenanigans are usually reserved for places further removed.

The wings are close to the action of the stage. So close, in fact, that in most theaters, if a performer tripped and fell awkwardly, chances are she would splat right onto the stage. Therefore, we treat the wings carefully, with respect. We know waiting in the wings is serious business.

Once, I quietly called to a fellow actor in the wings minutes before the curtain was to rise. I was going to tell him "break a leg," an expression of good luck in the theater. As he turned to me, tears rolled down his face. No, he hadn't just gotten bad news from home. He was preparing for his entrance—his first moment of light—where he appeared to the audience as a bereft son. I nodded and said nothing as the actor turned to continue preparing. He wasn't in his moment yet, but the almost-there-moment was so important that he would not cut short the waiting, preparing time it required. His waiting time was full of activity invisible *to* the audience, but crucial *for* the audience. He would give the role he had been called to play its full "wait."

The Disease of the Age

I'm sure we've all heard great sermons on the microwave instantaneousness of our modern lives, and how that "now" mentality has tinctured our lives in the kingdom. But as fast as our culture has changed in the last five years, the microwave analogy no longer holds two-minute boiled water. The microwave is a slow-moving mammoth compared to what we've got going on currently.

Now, "now" is not enough. It's not just that we desire everything now, but there is the additional pressure to *docu-*

ment everything now. (I post, therefore I am.) Post it *now*. Tweet it *now*. Instagram it *now*. Whatever moment you find yourself in must be curated, documented, and sent out into the world for consumption. Instantly. Who wants to know about that soul-lifting retreat you had last week? Why bother? Even the near past seems passé. And so the disease of "now" grows, and we have little herd immunity against it. We have all fallen ill.

We have lost our wait.

And many of us miss identifying and finding our light, our place in the Story, simply because we refuse to wait for it.

Wait Like Jesus

Kingdom stories operate on a different schedule, much to our chagrin and our near-pathological preoccupation with "now." God has no problem calling us to wait on him. He has no issue with placing us "in the wings," preparing and pruning us, giving us a sneak peek, but not an active role.

Many times every bone in my body called out, *Let me run. Let me go. Not yet*, God said. *Not just yet.* Your bones may be strong, kid, but those muscles aren't. There is work to be done. Work that remains unseen, but that is mission critical.

Charles Spurgeon, the gleaming preacher, said it this way:

If the Lord Jehovah makes us wait, let us do so with our whole hearts; for blessed are all they that wait for Him. He is worth waiting for. . . . The Lord's people have always been a waiting people.[1]

157

Even Jesus

Even the Light of the World, Jesus, didn't hopscotch past the divine waiting room. For three decades, for approximately 10,950 days, Jesus waited in the wings.

Do you ever ponder on what thirty years of waiting might have looked like for Jesus? Do you ever wonder what strength of character it took to hold himself back until just the right time? Once, I composed a "what if" monologue from the perspective of Jesus's sister. In it, she happens upon Jesus around the age of twenty-eight, walking in a field in the dead of night, asking his heavenly Father if his "now" is finally at hand. She marvels at his intimacy with God; she wonders at the oddity of his mission; she wonders who in the world this brother of hers really is. Interesting to imagine, perhaps, but the Bible remains largely mum on the specifics of Jesus's waiting time. What we do know is that he waited for the right time to enter the light of his Father. He waited for the right time to show up on the scene. He waited to be seen.

The only real glimpse we get of Jesus waiting in the wings happens in Luke 2. To set the stage: Jesus and his family have journeyed to Jerusalem for Passover when Jesus is all of twelve. After worshiping, the crew travels toward home—for an entire day. It is only then that they discover their preteen boy is missing. His parents search frantically, finally returning to the last place they saw him—Jerusalem's temple.

Let's pick it up in Luke:

The next day they found him in the Temple seated among the teachers, listening to them and asking questions. The teachers were all quite taken with him, impressed with the sharpness of his answers. But his parents were not impressed; they were upset and hurt.

His mother said, "Young man, why have you done this to us? Your father and I have been half out of our minds looking for you."

He said, "Why were you looking for me? Didn't you know that I had to be here, dealing with the things of my Father?" But they had no idea what he was talking about.

So he went back to Nazareth with them, and lived obediently with them. His mother held these things dearly, deep within herself. And Jesus matured, growing up in both body and spirit, blessed by both God and people. (2:46–52 MSG)

From this passage, how can you and I learn to wait—to prepare—like Jesus?

Wait actively. Sometimes we mistakenly equate waiting with thumb-twiddling, mind-numbing nothingness, very much like the interminable wait of the doctor's office (before smartphones entered the scene). And yet, over and over again, we see that it is not the waiting itself that matters as much as what we do with the waiting.

In the temple, Jesus's time of waiting is active and engaged. He is wide awake, listening and asking questions. (Notice the power of those questions again.)

In the Old Testament, the Hebrew word *qa-vah* is translated as our English word "wait." One of my favorite Scriptures is, "Those who wait upon the Lord will mount up on wings like eagles" (see Isa. 40:31). Learning of the ancient root of that Hebrew word has reframed my understanding of what waiting looks like in Jesus, because the root of *qavah* is from an archaic phrase meaning "to twine together," possibly as in rope making.[2] The very word—*wait*—carries within its meaning an *activity*.

While you wait, God's Word says that something of incredible value is being twined together. Twining together a strong rope takes time, but in the end you'll have something you can use. Something that will hold. Something of security and strength that will bear the *weight* of your *wait*.

Wait alongside. It's interesting that this sneak peek into Jesus's life before his earth-shattering debut is so full of—well, people. I wonder if I am the only one who thinks of waiting as a place of spiritual solitary confinement.

Yet in our Luke passage, we see Jesus determinedly pressing in to other teachers, leaders, and thinkers. In fact, he goes out of his way—leaving the crowd, leaving his family—to search out those who can help him in his journey of preparation. He doesn't wait in a vacuum. He waits alongside.

Finally, **wait appropriately.** Even though our preteen Jesus caused his parents' hearts to take up residency in their throats, the Scripture says he went home with them and listened to them. He waited well and placed himself under the shadow of the safest wings he could find at the time, those of his parents, and the heavenly Father they represented to him. And the Scripture says he grew in wisdom and maturity. And that wisdom and maturity would serve him when he finally took the stage of the ages.

Waiting on Big Red

One of the most challenging roles I ever played was Cassie in *A Chorus Line*. Cassie would have been large for anyone's wheelhouse, but it was humongous for mine. Remember, I was a back-row dweller; I was the girl who could dance passably, but a real-deal dancer I was not. Cassie demanded major dancing. And I possessed deeply uncooperative knees, to boot, knees that were always going one way instead of the other. They held all the way through the grueling choreography rehearsals. I can remember bracing them, babying them, and crossing my fingers.

We were days before opening night when, doing Cassie's big solo, I went into something as death-defying as a side lunge. (Sarcasm intended.) I felt the knee go pop. My kneecap had dislodged and was now on the side of my leg where no patella was ever intended to go. I remembered writhing under the dim wash lights as Sea, my director, rushed the stage. He was very calm. Somehow, through my sobbing, he stilled me and did what a good director has to do; he realigned the out-of-joint thing. All the actors came around me and lifted me to a car, which took me to a Greensboro emergency room. They discovered a serious ACL injury. For this particular injury I wasn't a good surgical candidate, so I was placed in a full leg cast. For six weeks, I was to be in the long, red tube. I called it Big Red.

The doctor assured me that I would be out of it in time to walk with my graduating class of 1988. Then I would have the summer to rehab for freshman year at Carnegie Mellon. Those six weeks were agony. I remember ticking them off in my calendar. Big red Xs to match Big Red. Nearing the end of the prescribed time, I remember thanking the Lord that I would get the heavy, itchy, stinky thing sawed off. I could taste freedom. I couldn't wait to see my hibernated leg.

The appointment proceeded well, the smell of sawed-open plaster like fresh-cut roses in my nostrils. There she was! My free, shriveled, hairy leg. (Sorry, folks!) The doctor did some prodding, some "hmm"ing, and then left the room. A bit later, he came back with a nurse accompanying him, with plaster and a tray of water that I knew too well. "Allison, I am so sorry. The knee is not ready yet. We need to cast it for another four weeks."

Tears ran like a faucet, as I pleaded with him to reconsider. What about walking at graduation? What about rehabbing and prepping for CMU? What about any option other than another cast?

He looked at me, undeterred. "Allison, I know it's hard to hear now, but the knee needs more time. You'll be glad we did this in the long run. You'll be glad we waited. Promise."

On went another cast. I walked at graduation in high-top Reeboks and Big Red. In another month, off it came, and I began the grueling process of rehab.

It is not lost on me that I never again suffered a showstopping knee injury. Not in four years of dancing every day in college. Not in almost 650 performances of a grueling dance show and countless other performances. In many ways, I was able to stand in the theatrical light as a performer because the knee held. And the knee held only because I waited.

Waiting Time in Jesus

Standing in the light God has for you sometimes means waiting. It might be months, like in my story with Big Red. It might be years, as it was for Jesus. It might be days and weeks as you wait on God's wisdom in prayer. There is no way around waiting in the wings, but what we do with it—oh, friends, that is very much up to us.

Waiting time in Jesus is never wasted time.

And our Jesus—and the light he calls us to—is beyond worth the wait.

Sparkler: Psalm 39:7 (KJV) says, "And now, Lord, what wait I for?" What are you waiting for? How have you found this necessary stage in Christian maturity? Is waiting easy for you? Why or why not? How are God and God's light for you worth the wait?

12

Being in the Moment vs. Stealing the Light

Let your manner of life be without covetousness,
being satisfied with the present.

Hebrews 13:5 BLB

Stealing the Light

Once, when I was just getting started as an actor, a fellow performer gave me some hard-knock advice. It was advice that I still chew on: The cast had been onstage for a rousing musical number, and in the blackout, we all exited into the wings. As we continued to move offstage into the stairwell, I could tell this man was sort of flummoxed with me. I approached him and asked if something was wrong. He said, "Allison, do you even know what you did?"

I shook my head, totally oblivious. He said, "You pulled focus. You upstaged me. Couldn't you tell?"

I apologized profusely, embarrassed. The truth of the matter is, I was so inexperienced that, no, I couldn't tell. I hadn't known I'd upstaged him. Obviously, I had drifted from my place over into his light, where he had been chosen by the director to be featured. Innocently, I had committed one of the theater's cardinal sins: I had stolen someone else's light.

You might wonder what in the world the big deal happens to be. Did the guy have such a big ego that a young girl's mistake bruised it that easily? Not at all. Actually, he was a kind gentleman, one who, along with his wife, regularly mentored younger performers. That day, wrapped in his sharp rebuke was a gift. By asking me if I understood that I had stolen his light, he was actually giving me a Christmas morning full of gifts. Gifts like these:

Whatever you do, remember that the story is king.

And that we are here to serve the story.

We are only in the spotlight because the story demands it.

Fighting to be seen when it is not your time or turn detracts from the story.

And if you steal the light—carelessly or purposely—you force the focus of the story from where it needs to be.

Another character's light is never your own.

You must know when the light is yours to inhabit and not.

In essence, my friend was saying: *Stealing the light is the very antithesis of actually finding it.*

Even as I write it, I have to sit with it afresh: stealing the light is the very antithesis of actually finding it.

How often have I been guilty of antithesis living? Of being tempted to steal someone's light in everyday life? Of inching closer to someone's God-given light, hoping that maybe, just maybe, it might reflect on me—just a smidge? When I do that, when I stubbornly step into someone else's light, I am effectively saying: *I want someone else's calling. I want someone else's timing.* And, most painfully and selfishly, *I want someone else's story.*

Anybody Else's Story

Remember middle school "career days"? I approached them with equal parts hope and dread. I liked them because they appealed to the creative slice of my brain, plus it was grand to "try on" roles to see if I liked the fit. During sixth grade, there was a gal who lived at the end of the cul-de-sac who was as close to a perfect specimen as the 1980s could have produced. She could have been the entire decade's muse. Not a frizzy curl or a wonky monogram in sight. Logoed and penny-loafered. Witty and magazine-pretty, she never had to worry about finding a bus seat partner, or anything else for that matter. She even did some part-time modeling. I wanted to be her; I'm quite sure I wasn't alone in that. So, for career day, I decided to be a "model" like her (can you smell the blood in the water?), but really, I was trying to be her. To the best of my young ability, I dressed like her, did my blue eyeliner like her, bought a shirt just like hers. I had my "model" down pat, getting up super early to don myself with the character. I remember that when I got on the bus to school and took my seat, I heard giggles and a voice saying, "Allison, what are you trying to be?" Immediately, I knew I had made a terrible choice, the shame blooming like nightshade in my heart, but I did have enough sense not to utter "a model" aloud. I remember stumbling over my words when I heard her whisper to her seatmate, "I think she's trying to be *me*." Sadly, she was right.

Snarky middle school girldom aside, this is a story I'm afraid all too many of us see ourselves in long into our twenties, thirties, forties, and beyond. Though we know Jesus doesn't want us running ourselves ragged chasing someone else's light or place in the story, we can't seem to help ourselves. We're stuck singing the musical theater ballad, "Someone Else's Story."[1] Even after years of walking with Jesus, I came face-to-face with the same schoolgirl from the bus—she was twenty-seven and sitting in a Greensboro pastor's office, frustrated.

By this time, I had left the show I had done in New York for several years and was entering into the long middle years as God was shifting parts of my story around. I remember sitting with my pastor, talking about how I desperately wished the Lord would send me "the one." I was desperate to be married. At twenty-seven, I felt old-maid syndrome was lurking. (Dramatic much?)

Even though I was feeling Jesus nudging me on to Nashville, on to another season, I pronounced to my pastor that I would not be moving. I would continue working in the temp office and helping coordinate the arts at his church. I even mentioned a couple of names of women I admired in the church who had lives that I wanted mine to look like. I told him I would simply be like them. Surely God would relent and send me a hubby.

My pastor looked at me, smiled, and let the silence fill the room after my barrage of words. We were friends, and he knew me better than I knew myself.

Finally, he said, "So, Allison, you just want to sit on the pew?"

I began to protest, and then he basically said, "Because that is the life you are describing to me. Life on a pew. You are telling me that you want to be someone else. You're telling me you want someone else's life."

He was saying to me that as much as I wanted somebody else's story or light, it would never work. Their story would never fit. Additionally, when God calls, God calls. The only sane answer is *yes*. He was saying that as a believer, my job was to respond to Christ's calling, not to pick a calling out like a piece of off-the-rack clothing, asking God to make it fit my frame as I ran off down the street in it.

Dear John, Dear Peter

Whenever you struggle with someone else's light or calling, you are not alone. John and Peter go before you. Have you ever paid much attention to the tension between these two in the Scriptures? There are curious mentions about one or the other's greater sprinting ability, who arrived first at the tomb, the belovedness and proximity of one or the other to the Savior. Maybe I am reading too much between the lines of the Book, but even a cursory look seems to suggest that there was more than just a friendly competition between these two apostles. In the end, the competition seemed to be laced with two very human concerns: closeness and calling. Closeness specifically to Jesus, as well as calling in the kingdom.

Seeing this struggle, my writer-hubby composed a song where he imagined what it must've felt like for John to watch Peter walk on water. Written in Jesus's voice to John, the lyrics have always put their musical finger on something deep in my heart:

> There's books to be written, John
> Now's not the time for a swim
> I know you wanna be just like Peter
> But there's a reason I didn't make you anything like
> him
> I know it's not clear to you
> Why I ask you two to do such different things
> But my memoir's being written even as we speak
> It's gonna be followed by the peasants and the Kings
>
> So, stay in the boat, John
> This water wasn't made for you to walk upon
> Stay in the boat, John
> You'll have a chance to prove your love for Me before
> too long[2]

Artistic liberty aside, there is little question these two jostled and hustled with one another's "light" in Jesus's story. Even after the crucifixion and resurrection of Jesus, Peter is still concerned with Jesus's plans for John, asking what is going to happen with John in the future (John 21:21). Jesus answers Peter's concerns with, "What is that to you? You, Peter. You follow me." John Piper makes an interesting observation about that moment: "Jesus' blunt words—"None of your business, follow me"—are sweet to my ears. They are liberating from the depressing bondage of fatal comparing."[3]

Amen and amen.

It intrigues me that Jesus ends the discussion with a *real answer* to Peter's inquiry. Not with specifics about John's destiny, but about Peter's. *The details of your destiny are in my hand. Nothing else matters. Peter, you follow me.* At its core, shining for Christ is ultimately a clarion call to follow Jesus. To follow Jesus into the moment he has for you, and not anyone else's. Nobody else's story is as exciting as the one Jesus is inviting you to.

Being in the Moment with Christ

Have you ever used the phrase "She's beside herself" to describe someone? We get it, right? The phrase is often used to describe a person not in control of her emotions. A woman "beside herself" is so out of control, it's almost as if she has abandoned her right mind.

For much of my life, I was a woman who lived "beside herself," but not because I was lacking in emotional temperance. I was lacking in emotional presence. Let me see if I can explain. Because of the disease of insecurity, I lived beside myself, critiquing myself, gauging my gains, anticipating my losses, hedging my bets. In essence, I was watching myself walk through life, like some critical observer. Like a woman by-the-side. I never had words for this feeling until I walked into a small prayer room in North Carolina over two decades ago, and heard two Christian ministers discussing this odd feeling. As I heard the two speak, I thought, *Aha! This has my name all over it.*

I was never really *in* the moment I was in. I was never fully in the moment with Jesus. I was always a little behind the moment—*Oh no, what I just said was so stupid*—or I was ahead of the moment—*Oh no, I hope they don't ask me what I think.* But I was never in the moment. I was rarely with the God who says of himself, "I AM WHO I AM" (Exod. 3:14). There is someone who walks alongside us, but it is never ourselves—it is Jesus. I had usurped Jesus as my walking partner and had replaced him with myself, trying to anticipate every social pitfall and pothole, rather than trusting Christ to do that.

Ironically, one of the first lessons we were taught in acting at CMU was the lesson of *being in the moment.* From freshman year to senior year, in any acting class we ever attended, this phrase was spoken, unpacked, and explored. We were taught, through a million different exercises, that believable acting first springs from being an actor so *aware—so there—so present to the moment you are in,* that truthful choices spring from that. Again, it was not about putting on the "show," but about showing up truthfully. If I had a crisp Benjamin for every time I heard one of my professors say to me or to another actor, "You're anticipating the moment. Just be in the moment you're in, Allison. Just be present in the now," I'd own a private island getaway.

It sounds so simple, but it is a difficult discipline—both onstage and in life. It is a discipline that takes time to work into our sinews and emotions. But, the longer I walk with Jesus, it is an ability I find myself improving in day by day, by his grace. I find that when I can be fully in the moment I am in—with Jesus—I stop madly chasing anyone else's moment. I don't possess a ravenous hunger for someone else's gift or calling. And that simple truth has helped me lose my appetite for someone else's light.

Who could've ever dreamed that over two decades ago—on a Pittsburgh campus—I had been receiving a master class in the things of the kingdom and hadn't even known it? It's a lesson I remember to this day:

If I stay in the moment with Jesus, there is more than enough grace for whatever the moment brings.

Leave the Moment to Him

I wish you could have been there. Not because it was tweet-worthy, but because it was so like the kingdom. It was a living parable of this truth:

Don't chase the spotlight. Chase Jesus, and leave the spotlight up to him.

My mother-in-law, Jetta Allen, is a unique woman. She wears the grace and presence of Jesus in winsome ways. Whenever she comes to church, I secretly grin watching the younger women casually line up to talk with her. Just this weekend I was at a shower when a gal said, "Well, I've been talking to Jetta." *Of course you have*, I thought, smiling. There is something about Jetta that draws others in—a radiant, overcoming heart that makes her words a flashlight to fellow path-walkers.

A particular visit a few months ago will forever be etched in my mind. It was the night Jetta ignited.

My husband, Jonathan, was preparing to lead an evening gathering at our church when he felt an urge to ask Jetta to pray a prayer of protection and wisdom over the students in attendance that night. His parents happened to be in town from North Carolina and Jonathan left a message with his request. As we were sitting in the front row, waiting for the night to begin, Jonathan walked down and handed Jetta the microphone. Jetta had a quizzical look on her face, which immediately communicated, "I have no idea why you are handing me a microphone." Jonathan reexplained what he hoped for her to do, as it was apparent that Jetta had not heard the message. She lightly demurred, but Jonathan was unmoved as he held the microphone out to her and she finally took it, waiting for the moment when her son would say, "Now's the time, Mom." Even though Jetta is not one to clamor to be the center of attention, she trusted God would suit her perfectly for the moment when it came.

The moment arrived about halfway through the gathering. Middle and high schoolers gathered as Jetta prayed. In a very tangible way, Psalm 145:4 was being lived out in prayer, "One generation will praise your deeds to the next. Each generation will talk about your mighty acts" (GW). It was one of the rare moments when, through quiet sniffles and a seventy-year-old's shaking voice, the weight of God's glory filled the temple. Heaven came low. The invisible seemed visible. The uncovered were covered. The unblessed were blessed. The banished were invited to the banqueting table. It was just one of those things.

Had you been there, you might have been struck by how the scene unfolded. Unlike what one might normally imagine, Jetta didn't take the physical stage to pray. She didn't climb the five steps, stand behind the pulpit, and wait for the glow of a warm wash to rise on her. She couldn't have, even if she had wanted to. Even with the faithful help of my father-in-law, Jim Allen, the steps would have been too much to manage. You see, Jetta has post-polio syndrome, and it is increasingly making movement—especially stairs—very difficult. When she goes out, she uses a walker or a scooter. In the 1950s, Jetta was in the last wave of kids hit with the paralyzing polio virus, just before the Salk vaccine made its debut. Her whole life has been a walking miracle. I mean that quite literally—the fact that she has moved as well as she has for as long as she has is a miracle.

After her stay in the hospital, like others who contracted polio, she rehabilitated. She learned to walk again. She went to college. She married, went on to have a teaching, social work, and later, a graphic design career. Jetta bore two sons and leads a vibrant, prayerful life in Christ. A life that led all the way to one of the spotlight moments of her life—her blessing-of-the-generations moment. It was a moment, by her own confession, that has been one of the most Christ-soaked of her life.

A spotlight moment that took place as she sat in the congregation.

You see, Jetta never chased anybody else's spotlight. *She chased Jesus and left the spotlight up to him.*

And when the time came, it was as if God said, "Daughter, I will move the spotlight to you. You sit right there in that holy chair and let my light rise on you. And when it does, breathe deep, Light-bearer, and confer my blessing on these beauties. You just be in the moment I bring and show up to the light I give."

And sitting in the front row, with God's spotlight upon her, Jetta did just that, becoming a living emblem of one of my favorite quotes, "Act well, at the moment, and you have performed a good action for all eternity."[4]

For all eternity, indeed.

Sparkler: For so much of my life, I was a spotlight chaser first and a Jesus chaser second, until he rescued me from that path. Can you relate to that statement? In what way? Are you, by nature, someone who is comfortable being in the moment, or do you relate when I speak of being "beside myself"? How so?

13

Understudy Graces

Imitate me as I imitate Christ.

1 Corinthians 11:1 GW

For my entire tenure of *Grease* on Broadway, I was a bit of an understudy chick.

I had a part that I played every night—Gertrude (we've already chatted about ol' Gertie), but I was also cast as the first cover (understudy) for three additional leads, which means that when one of the stars was out, I was on. Marty, Patty, and Ms. Lynch were in my regular performance rotation during the two years I was in the show. And I first learned to play them by understudying, which was a delightful spiritual discipline in disguise.

As a twenty-three-year-old college graduate debuting on the Great White Way (so-called because it was one of the first streets in the country to be illumined with electric lights), I was being given an education no money could buy, as I studied under actors far older and more experienced. I honed my own comic timing by understudying a master—a master who would go on to play a lead in a sitcom. I learned to trust my own wacky sense of physical comedy by watching a Tony nominee do the same. I watched. I observed. I found my way through being mentored by people far wiser, older, and more experienced than myself. I was a "number two" for a long season, and I am forever grateful. Being number two gave me guidance and permission to become a fully developed actor. It also protected me in the places where I wasn't ready for full scrutiny. Being a number two was protective.

And as much as egos can run rampant in any artistic world, this is one place where the theater gets it right. In the end, the needs of the story will trump the drive of the ego. "You need me on tonight as a lead? Great! You need me in the back row as my everyday character? Great! Whatever serves the story."

Number Two

At my son's school, we're required to display car tags in the pickup line. There are hundreds of students at the school, so those tags are the key to knowing which child matches which car. For many years, because our last name is Allen, our tag number was #2. I never thought much about it, until one day a friend said, "So, who's number one?" I told my friend I honestly had no clue. My friend joked he would have to know who number one was, lest he be driven batty.

Jokes and car lines aside, it seems we all want to be #1. A leader. Perhaps even The Leader. We want to be known as first adopters and pioneers. Go-to people. No longer honored to be a part of the team, we strain to be the star player. Being number two is fine enough only in that if we grind, we might one day land the number one position. This struggle to be primary is as old as humanity itself. Cain wanted to offer a better sacrifice than Abel. Diotrophes, in 3 John, is listed as a man who loved first place and did much to court and keep it. Even among Jesus's disciples, arguments flared up about who would be first. Check out the audacious request of John and James's mother, as she "humbly" asks for her sons to sit by Jesus's side when he comes into his eternal rule (Matt. 20:20–21)!

Aside from showing the very human side of the heroes of the faith, the Bible also shines a light on the blessedness of being in a supporting role, or a "number two." Joshua to Moses. Asaph and the Sons of Korah to David. Elisha to Elijah. Baruch to Jeremiah. On and on the lists go. Eventually some of those "number twos" are called upon to step into the primary position, as Joshua did for Moses. And as Elisha did for Elijah. But the others? The others were created to occupy, fully inhabit, and *enjoy* the position God had assigned them. This was God's light for them. As much as our often love-starved hearts long for the place of singularity, I have come to understand that many times the reason we long for a role of honor has nothing to do with God's glory and everything to do with our own. God, in fact, tells us to seek the place of least honor and leave the results to him (Luke 14:8–11). Our God-stages and the roles we play upon them are equally important but different in function and form. And when we can be okay with that, *truly* be okay with that, then we can know that maturity is saturating our hearts.

Supporting Roles

Ever had a few simple words slap you from slumber?

Having learned under some great preachers, I have had a million of those "word wake-ups" along the way. A particular awakening happened when I was all of nineteen years old in Fresno, California, preparing for my first trip as a musical missionary. I had taken a year off from Carnegie Mellon and had decided God was calling me to be a lifelong missionary. (Though that was clearly not the case, God wastes nothing— even our drastic detours. After that year, I would return to CMU and graduate.) But, back to the story at hand.

Our team's international outreach would be to Yugoslavia (before the country broke into brutal civil war). Our group would be the first missionary team in eons to present the gospel to prisoners, as well as offering open-air concerts for thousands of people at a time. Our vocal group would sing, and then a Yugoslavian believer would present God's good news in the language of the people.

Days were spent in musical rehearsals; nights were spent in spiritual formation. Speaker after speaker brought hard-won words of wisdom from the missionary field. I remember feeling like my newly-in-love-with-Jesus head couldn't take another wisdom firecracker. On one of the last nights, there was a man whose name I can't remember but whose words I will never, ever forget. He said something to us fresh-faced

Jesus chasers that has been a guiding light to me ever since. He said:

> You can never be fully released into your own vision until you learn how to be faithful in someone else's.

That wise speaker knew he was speaking to a chapel full of young men and women bursting with visions and dreams. He was spot-on. I, for one, was set on being the next missionary/contemporary Christian music star. Remember, this was the era when, if you had curly brunette hair and could carry an alto tune, surely you would be the next Amy Grant. Other young guns wanted to be the next Billy Graham or the missionary who finally infiltrated North Korea. We were a chapel full of dreams. And though those hopes and visions burned brightly within us, there we were, in California, raising our own support so we could wing our way around the world, singing for Jesus. And then came those words:

> You can never be fully released into your own vision until you can learn how to be faithful in someone else's.

One of my favorite Scriptures is the parable of the minas in Luke 19. A highborn man distributes some of his wealth to ten of his servants and says, "Make the money work. Treat it like you would treat your own." When the king returns, he rewards those who have been faithful with his money, and in return he gives them cities to rule that are—*don't miss this*—equal to the faithfulness they have demonstrated with the king's cash. The one who squirreled the king's money away, doing nada, is harshly judged. Many times this parable is used to teach stewardship of the gifts God has graciously given us, be they material or otherwise. But there is another prism through which to see the parable, and it really resonates with me: notice that the money was never the servants' money. Never. Not when it was given. Not when it was stewarded. Not when it was returned with interest to the king. However, because of their stewardship of the king's gifts, the servants were given their own. Don't miss this. The servants were faithful to another man's vision (*Make this money work!*), and in return they were given their own. (*Rule this city! Or five of them, why don't ya!*)

Not My Turn

It took everything in me not to dissolve into a puddle. But there were other people around, so I managed.

There I stood, outside the Greensboro art center, desperately scanning the *Godspell* cast list for my name. Surely there had been some kind of cosmic typo! How was it that I—a gal on the upswing—a gal who had started in the theater *because of Godspell*—who could sing every melody and harmony—who bled the musical if cut—how was it that that same gal's name was nowhere on the cast list?

But the evidence was all there in black and white: I had not made it.

I watched a couple of other elated performers initial their acceptance, while I managed a thin "Congratulations" and went back to the car where Mom waited to take me home to lick my ego wounds. I was bone-crushingly sad. Not just because my esteem had taken a whack—no one relishes "not making it"—but because *Godspell*, over any other piece, was the reason the theater had been a holy brush fire in my soul.

I was three or four when the pop musical broke upon the culture. As the Jesus movement of the 1970s was sweeping the nation, *Godspell* rode the wave. Young people—"hippies" especially—were coming to Christ in droves. Even "Day by Day," the show's simple anthem, was a hit on the mainstream pop charts. I remember making my gifted and brilliant father play the ditty almost every night on the piano for me. He always graciously obliged.

Though I didn't know it, Jesus used a 1970s pop musical to plant some pretty potent seeds in the soil of my four-year-old heart. Maybe that seems like a strange route to reach a heart—but God misses nothing and uses everything. Including out-of-the-box theatrical pieces.

Throughout history, theater has been used to trumpet the truths of God. The mystery and miracle plays of the Dark Ages traveled from town to town for hundreds of years, illuminating the Scripture because people couldn't read. Illiterate people encountered Truth because they saw Truth reenacted by actors. Even the Jewish feast of Purim—which commemorates Queen Esther's star turn before King Xerxes—includes a reenactment of the book of Esther, replete with costumes and hissing and applause.[1] The Bible records multiple times when God asked his prophets to enact spiritual lessons. Isaiah paraded around partially naked for three years, and Ezekiel was called to lie on his side for 390 days. The messages of

God to a wayward people could be clearly apprehended from such dramatic acts.

God, the Ultimate Creative, has always used creativity as a pathway to our hearts. And in my little life, he had used nothing so greatly as he used *Godspell*.

So, not making the show was about more than not making the show. It was about not making the show that had, in many ways, made me. All summer was a mopefest. I remember fitting ballet shoes at my job in the Dancer's Shop, wondering if rehearsals for the show were going well. I would try to catch wind of the girl who had gotten the role I so desperately wanted. I had seen her name on the cast list but didn't know her personally. Let's call it cleanly: I was young, immature, jealous, and a tad overinvested.

And then I got a phone call.

No, it wasn't *that* call. Not that last-minute, can-you-step-in-and-save-the-day-the-actress-has-been-non-fatally-indisposed-due-to-an-acute-food-allergy-anaphylaxis kind of call. But it was a call to serve, coming from none other than the director of the show himself.

"Allison, this is totally last minute. And I hate to ask, but we unexpectedly lost our spot operator for the show. Would you be willing to run the spotlight for *Godspell*?"

Oh. My. Stars.

Dazed, I heard myself saying, "Yes. Um. Yes, I think I can. Let me check with my parents, but I think I can." Permission granted. I showed up on the first night of tech week in my black shirt and climbed the fifty-two steps to the mezzanine of the Carolina Theater (which is actually the level above the balcony). Fifty-two long steps away from the stage. Fifty-two steps away from the role that was, at the time, my young heart's greatest desire.

I had never run a spotlight before and had to be taught. Not one thing about it was easy. Today's follow-spots are lighter and supported by modern technology. But back in the day? Running a spot was anything but easy.

The spot weighed hundreds of pounds, all of which moved seamlessly on a pivot but still had to be controlled completely by the (fifteen-year-old) person operating it. My greatest fear was that I would lose control of the beast and drop its weight, causing one thousand aggravated theatergoers to look up for the source of the crashing metal and the runaway spotlight. Beyond the physical demands lay the artistic ones. Catching the performer in the light was an exercise in hitting the bull's-eye with an arrow—in the dark—over 131 feet away. First, I had to learn to open the lens as stealthily as a cat and shine a two-foot crescent on the curtain far away from the audience's current focus. Then I had to throw the gel-colored iris wide open on the actor, an actor who I prayed to the Lord would hit their spot and find their light. Running a spotlight was hard and thankless—and absolutely critical to the story being told. It told the audience what part of the onstage story was most important at any given time.

You see, every time I spotlit the actor singing the song I desperately wanted to sing, playing the role I thought I had been born for, I was learning an important kingdom lesson: sometimes your place is in the light—and sometimes your place is to steward and support the light for someone else. Sometimes character development is more important than playing the character. Sometimes being faithful in what is a little thing to you (running a spotlight) will make you ruler of much (whatever light God ordained for us to inhabit).

From running the spot for someone else, I also learned that, in the kingdom, timing is everything. I wasn't *ready* for the role I desired. I couldn't command that stage. Not at fifteen. Not yet. It wasn't my turn, and leaning into that truth was liberating for me. I still had so much to learn—not just in my actor's craft, but in my heart. And I learned these lessons every night by focusing bright illumination on someone else. Humility and surrender grew deeper roots in the soil of my heart every time I threw the spotlight on her for her solo, a solo which was about laying down self-will and following Jesus all the way to the cross. Yes, indeed. As the days progressed, I found my overfrothed heart settling into peace. To my surprise, I found that I wanted the audience to fully see and experience her tender performance. I wanted the light on her to point to the Jesus she was singing about. I wanted to be faithful to the light (spiritually and artistically) that God had ordained for her.

Stewarding the light for someone else night after night, I learned that there is great and abiding joy when we can learn to celebrate someone else's victories. When we can throw a serious hootenanny because someone else wins! I wasn't throwing a party up there at all of fifteen years old, but I have learned to throw one since.

One of the deepest evidences in my life of the transformative work of Jesus is that he has helped me become more of a Psalm 20 girl. Psalm 20:5 says, "I will lift up my banners in the Name of my God when *you* are successful" (paraphrase). Usually, we lift up our banners when *we* are successful; we post and proclaim and pin. But this Scripture gives us a superior strategy. It nudges us to make a big deal of others' light in God. It nudges us to wave our spiritual flags when someone else experiences success.

I'll fire up my spotlight because you, my sister, are rising and shining for the King of All Glory. Celebrating you takes nothing away from me. Our God is big enough to go around. And I'm going to do everything in my power for you to be seen. Let's light you up!

That's a spotlight worth standing behind any day of the week.

Flip Side Light

There's a funny ending to the spotlight story, one that didn't fully click until I wrote this chapter. Less than two years after the entire swallow-your-pride-and-your-entitlement event, I would be playing the role of my dreams in *Godspell*. Different stage and direction, but I can promise you this: When I sat at Jesus's feet as the character and sang the song I'd longed to sing all my life, playing *the* role I'd longed to play all my life, it felt a little richer. It felt a whole lot more like the Jesus I was trying to make famous.

When the spotlight hit me from the light booth, I understood it from the flip side. I understood that grace is the same on either side of the story. Not one side of the light is more important than the other. Grace is the same, either way.

And it made me immensely thankful for the year it had not been my turn.

Sparkler: Have you ever been called to study under someone else? If so, what did you glean from learning under them? Did you experience grace in that second-place position? When have you been thankful it wasn't your turn?

14

The Places You'll Go

And he lighted upon a certain place, and tarried
there all night.

Genesis 28:11 KJV

remember the scene like it was yesterday:

Winter 1992.

Messy college apartment.

Disoriented, a Carnegie Mellon acting major awakens.

Overnight, Pittsburgh had been costumed in snow.

I woke up to the winter wonderland way past late, squinted
one-eyed out the window, and groaned at the snowy drifts.
Melt it. Please, Lord, just melt it. Nothing doing. My insides
turned slushy as I mentally clicked through my options. Walking was out. And I knew that my rear-wheel-drive beater

would never cut through all that snow. All the kitty litter in the world wouldn't give it traction. Plus, time had simply run out.

That was the exact moment my stomach crawled up my throat and sat down. I knew I would never make it to the theater on time.

In approximately one hour the curtain would rise on one of Carnegie Mellon's most ambitious productions ever: *Nicholas Nickleby. Nicholas Nickleby* was our competitive conservatory's beast of a senior production: a two-part, nine-hour show in which I happened to play five different characters. And one of those characters spoke some of the play's opening lines *in the opening scene*. I realized I was about to commit one of the theater's most cardinal sins.

I was about to miss "places."

Hold a Place for Me

"Places!"

That call means it's time to take your assigned position on the stage (or in the wings) for the opening of the show. The show's director has set each performer according to his vision, and as actors, our job, our *calling*, if you will, is to execute that vision.

From star to starry-eyed dancer, the minute the call to "places" rings out over the PA system, a perfectly choreographed dance begins. Bobbing and weaving like prizefighters, everyone who appears in the opening scene of the show moves efficiently and determinedly to get to their places.

If the actors don't get to their places, nothing else can happen. No heart-stopping opening dance-offs. No break-your-heart duets. No life-changing transformations. For all those transcendent, theatrical moments to occur, every performer and every crew member has to start correctly. And for both, starting correctly means we start in place.

I've heard the call of "places" close to a thousand times in my actor's life, and to this day, something in me snaps to attention when I hear it. No matter if I'm freaked out or worn out, I know exactly what to do when the "places" call comes. Like a ballet dancer's first position, or a mom's diaper-changing routine at 2 a.m., responding to a "places" call is muscle memory. When we occupy our place, the grand story can begin. The curtain can rise.

If you were to see it from the air—from somewhere, say, way up high on the catwalk (a passage above the stage, allowing access for hanging lights)—taking "places" would seem simple. Easy, even. But, man oh man, what it takes to get there.

Everyone Has a Place

Some of the most tedious rehearsals are those in which we block (or set) places. I can't tell you the number of hours I've been a part of a cast standing in abject quiet while the director sets onstage places for thirty or so actors. The director has gobs of considerations to juggle, so every actor knows that setting places isn't quick or done willy-nilly. Every actor understands that knowing his or her place is critical.

It's critical for us too.

Over a year ago, I was taking a power walk through Nehemiah, which happens to be one of my favorite Old Testament books. Nehemiah is drenched in capital *D* Drama: the righteous risk of rebuilding the gates and walls of Jerusalem while enemies who are as hungry as wolves lick their maws and crouch to pounce. The prevalence and prominence of prayer. The action, achievement, and advancement of a dispossessed nation. It's all there.

Oh, and one other thing: that great work takes place in fifty-two days in the midst of heckling, physical threats, and intimidation from enemy armies. It gets so hairy that Nehemiah instructs the people to work with a weapon in hand. And they do. Think of trying to build a house on an active battlefield, and you're coming close to the gritty, fast-paced narrative of Nehemiah. So imagine my surprise when I came across the great, seemingly boring pause of chapter 3, which is essentially a record of places. The entire chapter lists over fifty groups of people, as well as the portion of the wall or gate that is theirs and theirs alone to reconstruct. Verse 12 makes my estrogen-dominant self grin: "Shallum . . . ruler of a half-district of Jerusalem, repaired the next section with the help of his daughters." I just love that. Everyone had a place on the wall, as we are fond of saying in my faith community.

Everyone had a place. Even daughters. And God gave them that place to inhabit and work from—and even fight from if necessary.

God, it seems, is a God of place.

Put in Our Place

The expression "being put in your place" carries a feeling of being put down or put under someone's thumb. Oppressed.

Pushed down. Stuck. No one wants to be "put in their place" like that.

However, for an actor, the saying is comforting. It means something quite different. Being put in our "place" means that we know the director—like God through Nehemiah—has assigned us the most advantageous spot for us to begin our part of the story. Our "place" means we will be safe from moving set pieces. Our place is a place we can nestle into and launch from. We also know that no one else, no other actor, can stand in our place for us.

Rolling around the bottom of the soul of more than a few of God's daughters is a question. *"Do I have a place?"* Is there really a place designed by God for me to inhabit? It's a tender question that rises from a tender place. So many women struggle mightily to find their place, often mistaking their lack of "place" with people as a lack of "place" with their heavenly Father. Or perhaps they stood in a place that God never intended until it drained them of vitality and joy, all because someone else expected it of them. Or they expected it of themselves. And now they question the whole idea of a "place" altogether. They feel unmoored, as if the anchor has been cut and they drift from situation to situation in search of their "place." I want to assure you that everyone has a place in Christ—hidden in him (see Col. 3:3).

And I believe that if we will lean in close to his heart, like John did at the final supper, we will hear his whispers. He desires to pick us up gently and put us gracefully into our place. I think of the Scripture that says, "The boundary lines have fallen for me in pleasant places" (Ps. 16:6). If our seasons and times are in his hand (Ps. 31:15), surely so is our place. Our great God is a God of place and placement.

Even in heaven, Jesus is actively preparing a place for you and me (John 14:3).

Changing "Places"

John the Baptist stood unapologetically in God's place for him.

When the time came, he was more than willing to be seen—wild attire, honey and locusts, and all. He was the master of ceremonies, proclaiming repentance and preparation for someone else—the Christ—who was yet to come. He was the prophesied messenger of Malachi. He had been named by an angel. Filled with the Spirit in the womb. First cousin to Jesus. Talk about a heavenly spotlight.

In ministry he had drawn huge audiences. He had been given a megaphone voice with which he bellowed, "Prepare ye the way of the Lord," and people dove into the waters and came up different. John was the principal player God was using in the eternal Drama. Crowds and contrition, center stage.

And yet in John 3, when John the Baptist's disciples come bringing the report that Jesus is now baptizing his own disciples and that everyone is running after him, John is the very picture of graciously understanding that something about his place is changing. *He is changing places.*

Instead of defending his position or mounting a Facebook PR campaign decrying this moving in on his territory, he says to his hot-under-the-robe disciples, "You yourself know I told you that I am not the Christ but have been sent to testify about the Christ. The bride [the people] belong to the bridegroom [Jesus]. I'm thrilled to hear his voice rising on the scene. My joy carries me away. He must become easier to see. And I? I must become more obscure" (John 3:28–30, paraphrase).

John the Baptist then goes on to say some of the most fascinating words of Scripture. "The one [Jesus] who comes from above is above all; the one who is from earth [himself, John] belongs to the earth, and speaks as one from the earth." In very poetic language, John is declaring that Jesus's place is above all, because he comes from above all. Continuing, John says that his own "place" is from earth and that he speaks as one from earth.

John here is declaring the preeminence of Jesus's place in God's great story. He is also declaring that Jesus's place is greater than his own. Heaven is greater than earth. Jesus's place is heaven and earth, John's is earth—and because of that, John says it is time to decrease, time to step out of the spotlight and step aside as God in human skin fully enters the scene.

John knew and fully inhabited his particular and peculiar place, until he knew that God had changed it.

Grace for the Place and the Pace

I have often heard it said that when the grace (God's enabling power) lifts from a particular place, it is time to move on. At the end of two years in New York, living any young actor's dream, I sat in a stairwell, observing my fellow cast members enter and exit their particular scenes. A certain knowing had been growing for a while, but that night the knowing snuggled up to me like a goldendoodle who wasn't leaving until I scratched its belly. I sensed the Lord's internal prod, "It's time to go, Allison. My grace has lifted for you in this place."

Now, mind you, relationships weren't strained. Performance wasn't in question. I had been there for two years and valued the opportunity and honored the work. It wasn't as if things had suddenly gone south. Not at all.

But that night I felt the Lord pulling up stakes and prepping me to "move on"—and I knew I had to follow him, no differently than when the children of Israel had to move as the cloud and the pillar of fire representing God's presence did. He was changing my place, and the safest thing I could do was move when he moved. Even if that meant leaving behind Broadway, the opportunity of a lifetime for an actor. However, I could sense a season change, and along with that, a change of place. So I moved. Back home.

The first Sunday I was home I walked into my home church, Grace Community Church, and as I entered I saw this lanky, floppy-haired man going after God with a guitar. He played the instrument like he might break it. He sang the words like proclamations, as if his midnineties, flannel-attired heart might crack open with the holiness of God. This was no performance. This was a man, like John, whose own heart leapt when he heard the voice of Jesus. He burned for the bright Morning Star up on that stage. I admit, I took notice.

Originally, I had meant for Greensboro to be a watering hole for a tired gal. Greensboro was a pit stop. Greensboro couldn't be my place, could it? However, it was clear that the Lord was stirring the waters, saying, "Stay here, Allison. This is your place geographically and spiritually for a while. *I am here.*" I pitched my tent and stayed—with his grace.

I scored a job at a temporary staffing company and dug in, Broadway in the rearview, at least for the time being. In eleven months, through a series of God-setups and the machinations of our oldest friend, Lori—Jonathan (that lanky guitar player) and I would have our first date. I can remember thinking, "Thank you, Jesus. A man with whom I can wear heels!" Crazy about the boy, I knew when he danced with me as the credits rolled in the empty movie theater on our first date that I was a goner. We would be married nine months later. We would move to Nashville immediately. I was sure the next place—Nashville—would be God-adventure upon God-adventure.

And it was, just not in the way I dreamed.

On the Shelf

For the next seven years, the place God had for me was largely "on the shelf." During that season, God relentlessly dug up major roadblocks and unfelt pain. He set down roots in my marriage. He gave me a huge B12 shot of spiritual rest, restoration, and realness. My "place" on the shelf lasted right up until we had our first child, Levi. I wasn't "on the shelf" because of any major moral failing or some stubborn sin issue, but because there were things I had to learn that only being on the shelf with Jesus could teach me. After years of performing for a living, which is, by nature, a very public thing, I needed a "place" of unwitnessed use to the kingdom. I needed a "place" where the only light on me was the light of his face (Num. 6:25), and perhaps the few people here and there whom he ordained as witnesses to that light. He was still using me—now it was just in a nearly invisible role, rather than in an always visible one. Not one bit less important than the times I had been in the spotlight. After so many years of pressure, it was an unspeakable relief to be in a different place, geographically and spiritually. To experience the relief of the light and easy yoke Jesus promises. I lived at the crossroads of Quiet Street and Anonymity, happily.

After we married and had moved to Nashville, I scored a retail job at Laura Ashley. (I have some floral beauties hiding in my linen closet to prove it.) I sang on the worship team of a church plant, standing by Jonathan's side as he stepped more fully into the role of worship pastor. We co-led a college and career Bible study with another couple out of which would hatch tons of beautiful, fledgling fireflies of the kingdom.

Also during this time, I began to teach on the collegiate level, as well as privately—coaching young acting hopefuls and even celebrities and athletes who needed to learn to tell their stories in public more vibrantly. And then I began to write for them. All very behind-the-scenes stuff. Stewarding the spotlight for someone else. During those years I functioned as a bit of a Christian Cyrano de Bergerac (a character who anonymously wrote love letters for his friends who couldn't quite get their words to flow). I was changing places.

Taking a gander at those years on a holy shelf, I want to break out the 1990s albums and do the electric slide, because I learned a primary lesson—one that I carry with me, no matter where I stand, no matter where I am seen, whether that light is a spotlight or a dim glow. Those seven years taught me that while personal achievement seems to be the dominant currency of the culture, personal surrender is the dominant currency of the kingdom. Those years taught me to surrender.

Those seven years on the shelf taught me to surrender to the God of place. And pace.

. . . And Off Again

After seven years—ironically, a number for completeness in the Bible—something momentous happened, though I wouldn't have recognized it at the time. My visionary pastor and dear friend, Steve Berger, said to me, "It's time. It's time for *Magdalene*." God used him like a holy match.

Magdalene was a play I had begun to write at Carnegie Mellon University years earlier. Through his encouragement, we added music and mounted the musical, offering it at church. The response was overwhelming, as God seemed to use a first-time playwright's wonky offering in his hand like an arrow. We were astounded at the personal stories of healing and redemption. One anonymous person even left a designer bag full of drugs, obviously ready for selling, under her seat. That's only one redemption story among a slew of them. Only God.

Unbeknownst to me, someone attached to a vibrant women's ministry attended a production (one in which I played the title role, if only because we had just ten days to mount it) and thought that I would perhaps be a fit for doing drama with Women of Faith. Through another set of God-circumstances, I wound up pinch-myself happy doing one-woman pieces around the country.

Because of those three years, I was able to begin speaking and teaching around the country, which is what I gleefully do now. Sometimes I do drama pieces, many times not. Many times I only speak. But I see God's hand in it all. I see that he got me here—from there. Ironically, after so many years, I wound up back on the stage, inhabiting the light of Christ differently, more settled, more surrendered. More ready for Jesus to be the easiest thing in the room to see, without my secret name devouring my heart and those character shoes cramping my Jesus style.

Perhaps the safest thing I ever did was trust God's place and pace for me. I recognize every pit stop, every wait in the wings, every seven-year intermission, every understudy opportunity, as a part of the pilgrimage. And I remember that God uses everything and wastes nothing. I also remember that God is a better door-opener for us than we could ever be for ourselves—and it is always better to wait for the door God opens than to strong-arm one open for yourself. In this regard, all God ever asked of me, or any of us, is to trust his timing and to step into the moment he brings.

So often in our society, we are taught that our life's trajectory should continue up and up, like an arrow whizzing toward the bull's-eye of the sun itself. I've always said, however, that the journey of walking with Jesus and following him into the light he provides has been more like the up and down of a heartbeat on an EKG. There is always vitality and activity, but sometimes it's mountain high, and sometimes valley low.

Walking with Jesus is like the rhythm of a heartbeat.

A Last Place Heart

One crisp morning about six years back, I happened to be watching my son Levi ride his bike in his school's annual field day extravaganza. With a cheer, we sent the students over the starting line as they pedaled hard against inertia. In only a matter of laps, I watched as Levi slid to last place in the fourth-grade competition. I watched with a little pinch in my heart, wondering how he felt to be bringing up the rear. I confess, I may have even said to another bystanding parent, "His tires are a little low on air, I think."

On and on the laps went, as we parents chatted on and off, clutching coffee thermoses and throwing sideways glances at our racing children. After a moment, another parent nudged my arm, bringing the most quizzical thing to my attention: Levi swerving lazily in time to the song that was thumping on the speakers; Levi singing the lyrics as he went by; and finally, Levi chanting with every bit of his outsized heart, "I LOVE LAST PLACE! I LOVE LAST PLACE! I LOVE LAST PLACE!"

For laps and laps he chanted it like it was the best news in all the world. Another parent bopped by, mentioning with a smile, "Do you know that Levi is chanting that he loves last place?" I said, "Yeah—I, uh, I see that." I'm sure I shook my head a bit, understanding I was witnessing something very interesting, if not downright remarkable.

Levi had opted out of the competition. He'd chosen to make the ride worth taking.

He'd courted contentment and caught it. He'd made joy his traveling partner and kicked comparison to the curb. He'd decided that last place didn't have the right to define him. In fact, if last place was his place for the race, he was going to make the most of its rare and unusual joys.

On a bike, with a chant in his mouth, my boy schooled me afresh. Oh, Lord, give me a heart like Levi in last place.

"Places!"

By the way, I got to my place. My place in the senior show, that is.

A friend with a much more snow-worthy car came to the rescue, getting me to the theater with minutes to spare. I remember barely pinning my wig to my head, stumbling into my 1800s costume, getting my mic set up, and running to the stage like a Carolina girl running barefoot for the ocean on a 100-degree day. I made it with a couple of minutes to spare. Against fierce odds and fiercer snow, I found my place. The tiny glow-in-the-dark X marked my spot. I stood on it, grateful to be there. I prepared to play my role in the drama. I had made it, just in the nick of time.

I took a deep breath, gathered my wits, and watched as the curtain rose and the lights came up.

I was in the right place.

I was home.

Sparkler: Do you believe that Jesus has a place for you? A unique place of radiating for his glory? Have you ever longed for someone else's place? If you feel as if you have never quite had or found your place in Jesus, may I suggest something? Would you begin by sitting at the feet of Christ, like Mary of Bethany, and just being with him, asking him about that? What does he speak to your heart there? Daughter, be assured: you have a place.

15

Despite the Critics

Do not be afraid; you will not be put to shame.
Do not fear disgrace; you will not be humiliated.

Isaiah 54:4

When you step into God's light for you, expect criticism.

I didn't like writing that sentence any more than you liked reading it, I bet. In fact, I have spent much of my adult life magically wishing those ten words away. I wish they weren't true of life on God-stages or theatrical stages or any stages. But they are.

However, those words are true for you and me, and they've been true for God's people from at least the book of Genesis. Here's just a small smattering.

A Critical Compendium

Joseph also told his father about this dream, but his father **criticized** *him.* (Gen. 37:10 ERV, emphasis mine)

The people there **criticized** *the blind men and told them to be quiet. But they shouted more and more, "Lord, Son of David, please help us!"* (Matt. 20:31 ERV, emphasis mine)

So when Peter went up to Jerusalem, the circumcision party **criticized** *him* . . . (Acts 11:2 ESV, emphasis mine)

It is this last verse that has me coming in for a closer look.

The Greek word rendered "criticized" in Acts 11:2 is a form of the word *diakrinō*. When you look deeply into its meaning, *diakrinō* has multiple definitions, including "to go back and forth thoroughly" and "to judge/discern." But it is that "back and forth" part that has me leaning in, because to *diakrinō* (criticize) someone or something can mean to judge and discern correctly, or—get this—it can mean to over-judge and go too far in critique, as was almost certainly the case in Acts 11:2. It all depends on context. The word is used both ways. Sometimes the criticism is accurate and fair in its assessment, and sometimes it overreaches and over-judges, as is the sense in the verses above.[1]

Constructive criticism brings course correction and, taken to heart, can put courage in. Destructive criticism often dislodges us and takes courage out. Destructive criticism is the kind that no one sets out the silverware for, and yet it's the kind of criticism that is coming over uninvited for breakfast, lunch, and dinner. And it's the kind I want to talk about here. Especially now, since anyone who has a computer and knows how to clack the keys can join the ranks of "critic."

It makes stepping into God's light a fearful proposition. I definitely get that.

Critic-Free Zone

I used to fantasize about a theater without critics. I even had a super-original name for the theater company: "Theater without Critics." Way to be known for what you're against. Plus, that is one hooky title.

My thinking was that this bold, experimental theater company would exist only in the space of whatever real exchange happened between an audience and the production itself. Our new company wouldn't court critics or press to come review whatever show we were producing. We knew we might miss out on glowing reviews, but we would also miss the glowering ones. We would simply let each production rise and fall according to the audience's experience of it. If the audience guffawed and grabbed tissue, great. Word would spread. People would follow. If the audience gave pity laughs and filed out in a stupor, well then, we would know we missed the mark artistically and would double down next time. This pipe dream was my naïve attempt to fix a problem that I have witnessed as long as I have done anything in the public eye: the oftentimes withering power of overly judgmental, public criticism of projects and people.

Especially when stepping out in the light for the first time.

Now the stuff of urban legend, the first reviews in 1985 of the musical *Les Misérables* live on in collective memory. You can find transcribed copies of them here and there on the web, but suffice it to say, words like *turgid* and *sentimental* dot the paragraphs like inky, acid raindrops. It is a wonder the show survived the first wave of negative press to go on to be the absolute sensation it has since become. The story continues: the next day, so goes the legend, the phones at the London theater rang off the hook as people tried to score tickets for the new show. The piece had hit a collective public nerve and would go on to be one of the most beloved pieces of musical theater ever. Some critics, in this case, missed (or dismissed) the palpable connection between the Drama and the hearts of the audience.

Though my "Theater without Critics" idea would never grow from a "brain hurricane" to make landfall, I see now that I was trying to find a creative solution to one of the more painful possibilities about stepping into any light, particularly God's light: overly judgmental criticism and how closely it feels like its first cousin—rejection.

It's Personal

Having personally experienced the sting of public criticism, I can tell you it is no tiptoe through anyone's tulips. At the time of occurrence, it felt positively soul-scarring. It may have taken a lot of long drives with loud music to recover. During those drives, when I finally turned down the noise, I had to do battle with who (or Who) had the final say over my life. Who got to weigh in. I had to pursue maturity more deeply and stare honestly at the criticism, as well as any merit that might be there. I had to take in the constructive criticism and "spit out the bones." When the criticism was overreaching, I had to wrestle with whether the critic's pen or God's providence would have the final say. Through God's grace, I slowly exited the noisy car and reentered my life. Even as I did, I had to ask myself if I would get back into the runner's crouch to race again, or exit the track altogether. It was not a glib fight, I assure you. Overjudmental criticism can leave you sidelined, sucking wind, wondering if you ever should have stepped out in the first place.

Personally, I have known people whose dream and ministry wings have been seriously clipped by overly judgmental criticism. People who never really put themselves out there again. People for whom a brutal critique left a lingering bruise that never healed.

And perhaps more eternally significant, I have known daughters of God who have never stepped into their light for fear of what "they" (the critics) might say. I have also known daughters who once stood bravely in God's glow for them—who once knew what it meant to dare to step out—but have since retreated from their place because of negative, overly judgmental criticism.

That criticism might come from the aforementioned unknown "they"—or from those who share your coffeemaker. No matter the source, the effect is often the same. Overly judgmental criticism extracts internal fortitude with dizzying speed. And in reaction, some of us have flat-out decided that we will not be children of the light, not if the price we pay is negative criticism and its bosom bud, rejection. It is simply too painful.

Many of us would rather dwell in the shadows than dare to shine in Christ. Not if daring to shine means being criticized.

When I was coming up, criticism existed on ink and paper—and only existed for a time. Those criticisms had a life, certainly, but that life was relatively short in the scheme of things. If someone eviscerated you in paper and ink, eventually that paper would disintegrate, or be used to pack someone's nice china for the movers. Eventually, very few people would recall the words of a poison pen.

Now, however, these critical elements can live on ad infinitum. Let us pause to thank "the inter-webs," as my hubby calls it. Unfortunately, there is little we can do to slow the ease with which it flows. The toothpaste is out of the tube. The critical tide will not be ebbing. Anyone can be a critic, it seems.

We have to live with it, friends, but perhaps we can learn to live with it a little bit differently. And the first step to living with criticism differently, I believe, is to understand who is *not* criticizing you. Who is *not* an overly judgmental, condemning critic of you or your life.

*The One who is **not** a critic is Jesus himself.*

Not a Critic

Earlier in the chapter entitled "Trusting the Director," I mentioned a difficult technical piece I did in my final year with Women of Faith. It was a piece in which the main character, Annie, has a loopy nightmare where she is constantly being judged for her dance ability, though she is no dancer. The three judges brutally critique her ability, her appearance, her performance—even rewarding her with the show's lowest score in history, a negative five. Annie hops back up and tries again, trying to extract a positive critique from the judges. After Roger-Rabbiting herself into a flop-sweat frenzy on the dance floor, Annie comes to understand that it is impossible to please someone who has already determined they will not be pleased. In other words, she cannot win the war she is finding herself in.

Finally, Annie cuts off the judge's barrage of snarky body-shaming and soul-marring criticism with this:

> Enough! That's enough! First of all, I never asked to dance on this show. And, second, I never asked to be judged by you, because, well because . . . you guys are not my judges. Not you and not the world and not even the critic inside my own head. There's only One Person who gets to weigh my life and His Name is Jesus, and He doesn't watch every move I make to see if I'm doing it wrong, or if I could do it just a little bit better, or kick a little higher. He doesn't sit on the sidelines with a scorecard in His hands.
>
> He's not a critic!

Not in one list of all the incredible names of our Jesus do I find a place that calls him a critic. Nowhere. Certainly he is called the righteous Judge (2 Tim. 4:8) and one day will judge all things, rightly, with truth and justice. But he is not an out-to-get-ya overly judgmental criticizer.

Jesus's heart of correction toward us feels nothing like the driven pointedness of harsh criticism.

Settle into this, sister: Jesus is not a critic of your life. He doesn't sit on the sidelines with a scorecard in his hands. And knowing this will lead you to dare to step fully onto the God-stage he is inviting you to. You will not arrive in heaven and be presented with a stack of newspapers or a spreadsheet critiquing every little move you made.

You will run into the arms that have cheered you on since the day you said yes. Who ordained every one of your days—in his Book—before one of them came to be (Ps. 139:16). You will run to the One who whispers in your ear, "Well done, good and faithful servant" (Matt. 25:23).

A Holy Immunization

One of the things that has assisted me in tucking criticism into its proper place is something Jesus pressed into my heart during difficult seasons in my life. In times where there has been no discernible outward growth and no large fruit, he whispered something astonishing: *You please me, Allison.*

You please me, daughter.

I admit, at first I recoiled against that intimate and tender phrase. Kind words are sometimes difficult for me to allow into the inner chambers of my heart. (I'll be talking about this in my next counseling appointment.) It felt too intimate, too tender. And it left me skeptical. Truthfully, I felt as if I was displeasing him, and here he came, whispering the very opposite to my heart. That I pleased him greatly. That just by being in Christ, I pleased him.

There had to be a catch, right? Something like, "You please me, daughter, so please try a little harder."

As a gal with an overdeveloped work ethic, this was a big ol' horse pill to swallow. The scaffolding of my life—even my life in Jesus—was that you had to work, earn, fight, accomplish, achieve. But I took in these strange words, and over time, I realized that this truth is the beeping home base icon on the GPS. It is because of Jesus, because of his sinless life, and his completed work on the Hill of the Skull, and his "death doesn't get the last word" rising three days later, that I have been given everything—including the Father's deep pleasure.

I began to realize that, somehow, I lived from God's guaranteed pleasure—that if he was pleased with Jesus, he was pleased with me, because I was hidden in Christ. In theological terms, this is called the doctrine of justification. As Brennan Manning says so poignantly in his book *The Raga-muffin Gospel*, "My deepest awareness of myself is that I am deeply loved by Jesus Christ and I have done nothing to earn it or deserve it."[2]

I suddenly saw that I couldn't make him more pleased with me if I tried. In fact, I believe that was the lesson he was trying to teach me: *You can stop trying so hard, daughter. You can get off the wheel. Abandon the war. Wave the flag. Quit the "show."* He seemed to be saying, *Live life knowing you already please me, rather than living life trying to avoid displeasing me.* The motivation is different and so is the fruit. And life in Christ becomes a lot more fun, and free.

And that freedom—that is a gold-standard immunization against the withering power of overly judgmental criticism. Because ultimately, if we meditate on and cherish the idea that his judgment of me is "pleased," then we are immunized against the fear of overjudgmental criticism. Luke's Gospel says it this way, "Do not *be afraid*, little flock, for your Father has been *pleased* to give you the kingdom" (12:32, emphasis mine).

What else can man do to that most hidden part of me? I will not fear being "confounded and put to shame" (see Isa. 54:4), because his verdict is in: pleased. Stamped on the stuff of my life, like a maker's indelible mark.

That's going to give you a B12 shot for what we'll chat about next.

No Matter What

Do it. Even when criticized.

Yep, I don't adore those five words any more than I adored the first ten at the top of this chapter. But I believe them just as much.

Just as *Do it afraid!* has become a cultural catchphrase, I think *Do it. Even when criticized!* should be as well.

There are going to be tummy-turning times when the wrong kind of criticism comes. When the words of over-judgment—be they personal or public—are inked into your mind like a tattoo. When someone is going to think it is their God-given place to take you down a notch or two. (Remember, I'm talking about destructive, overly judgmental criticism, not the constructive sort.)

When those words come, remember, your Father's right critique is that he is pleased with you. Like the ultimate Director, he stands for you. And those overly judgmental words?

Well, they hit him first. They pass through his hands, and it will be his hands that hold you up when your knees buckle.

Daughter, because of my Son, you couldn't please me more. Don't leave your place. Don't abandon your light. Take another step.

Doing it criticized, my friend, may be one of the most authentically brave things you will ever do.

Doing It Criticized

The book of Nehemiah is one made-for-the-screen epic. In it, Nehemiah has been tasked with rebuilding the walls of Jerusalem. The Israelites are met with numerous challenges along the way—political, logistical, and most pertinent to this chapter, critical.

During the holy reconstruction, the faithful people of Israel have stationed family groups along the walls like sentinels. Alternating between dagger and trowel, they keep rebuilding the wall. Because threats and curses haven't caused the people to turn tail and run, Nehemiah's enemies, the Terrible Trio (Sanballat, Tobiah, and Geshem), have tried luring Nehemiah into the plain of Ono for a "talk." (Some commentators believe the Terrible Trio were planning on weighting Nehemiah's ankles and tossing him into the closest body of water.)[3] Nehemiah basically gives them a "no can do" on the Ono invite and keeps on keeping on, telling them, "I am engaged in a great work, so I can't come. Why should I stop working to come and meet with you?" (6:3 NLT). Nehemiah is a wise enough gluten-free cookie to know these men are being used by the enemy to draw him out of his

213

light, to distract him from his task. Four times they employ this ruse. Four times it fails.

Getting desperate, the Terrible Trio have to devise a new plan to grind Operation Rebuild to a halt. They pick up their poison pens and let the words fly. They send a mendacious, openly critical letter of Nehemiah throughout the land. And when I say open, I mean open. An open letter in that day and age was especially insulting; commentators say that the ugly contents were specifically meant to be spread near and far.[4] Hence the "open" thing. Sanballat's letter is an ancient version of criticism gone viral. Anyone who wants to read it just has to click on their Twitter feed. It's everywhere—like kudzu. (I happen to be writing this during the summer presidential campaign season, when I am watching internet criticism behave like kudzu on Miracle-Gro.) But back to Nehemiah and his letter.

The critical letter attacks Nehemiah's character, his intent, his spiritual integrity. The epistle even claims that Nehemiah's endgame is to elevate himself over the king. Those are head-lopping words. Every critique is false, every word is a lie, but as is so often the case, who needs the truth when an inaccurate overjudgment is so much jucier? Clearly, this Terrible Trio will stop at nothing to halt the work.

Finally, the letter's contents reach the ears of Nehemiah, and he simply and succinctly replies, "There is no truth in any part of your story. You are making up the whole thing" (6:8 NLT). Just like that. Nehemiah says, "I assess your poisonous criticism of me, and this work, and my verdict is, 'Not true.'" Nehemiah continues writing his story, saying, "They were just trying to intimidate us, imagining that they could discourage us and stop the work. So I continued the work with even greater determination" (6:9 NLT).

He assesses the bullying and gets back to building. In fact, the Scripture seems to say it actually fuels him to work with greater or increased determination. The ridicule makes him rise. As they continue the work of building the fortifying wall, I think of the lyrics of the hymn "A Mighty Fortress Is Our God." In it, Martin Luther declares,

> For still our ancient foe
> doth seek to work us woe;
> his craft and power are great,
> and armed with cruel hate.

Boy, howdy, is that ever the case when faithfully carrying on the work God has called you to. The cruel hate of "haters." Luther goes on,

> The prince of darkness grim,
> we tremble not for him;
> his rage we can endure,
> for lo, his doom is sure;
> one little word shall fell him.

I wonder what word Nehemiah used to fell the enemy behind the brutal, critical attack. Maybe it was a holy "no," as he picked up his tool and refused to leave his light due to criticism.

Nehemiah's story is a spiritual master class for *doing it criticized*!

Quack and Roar

I was in upstate New York when a phrase popped into my head. (We'll get to the phrase in just a minute. I promise.) In the particular moment, I was leading a conference session for creatives about leading creatives. We were discussing all the attendant joy and challenge that come with leading those who sometimes carry significant brokenness along with all that outsized beauty.

The Q&A session went on like they tend to do. And then the atmosphere shifted a bit. To me, it felt as if realness surprised us like a God-kiss on the brow. All of a sudden the question wasn't just, "How do we do it?" but "How do we maintain our hearts while we do it? We're called to this work, this leadership 'light,' but how do we maintain our hearts in the process?"

I looked at those beautiful faces—people who tenderly stewarded the beautifully broken gifts of those entrusted to them—and many seemed weary. Some of the questions even revealed the spiritual fatigue of the participants, due to painful criticism of them as leaders and volunteers. Maybe even the overly judgmental type of criticism. None of us in the room hailed from the city of Perfect. As people or leaders, we all were aware of our deep inadequacy. To be clear, there was neither a sense of self-aggrandizement or victimhood. These weren't thin-skinned, prickly people—people who withered at the first hint of conflict or criticism. These were faithful people, constrained by the love of Jesus and serious about serving his bride. Alongside that love, though, there had been a particularly difficult enemy at work: nagging criticism. From within, from without, from the enemy himself.

"How do you do it, Allison?" someone asked.

And then the phrase popped out of my mouth.

"Duck's back. Lion's heart." I continued, "I mean, when criticism comes, I think we have to ask Jesus to help us cultivate a duck's back and a lion's heart."

Developing a duck's back simply means that when something painful—perhaps overly judgmental criticism—tempts you to abandon God's light, make the decision beforehand to allow it to be like water off a duck's back. One fine way to do that is to decide ahead of time what you will *not* do when criticism comes: Don't memorialize the pain. Don't coddle or cuddle the criticism. Don't be quick to be offended by it (Matt. 10:14). Don't pick it back up. As much as is humanly possible, let it roll off your back, like water off a duck's back.

And, remember, sisters, the time to make that decision is *now*. Beforehand. Not in the middle of a critical firestorm. Talk to Jesus about these things now.

Remember what Nehemiah does when the poisonous letter's contents finally reach him? He says, simply, "There is no truth to what you are saying. You are making the whole thing up." In that moment, Nehemiah is being like a duck. He's had some practice with critics, mind you. I believe he's already made his decision on how he will respond. By the time we get to the letter, we are on the fifth round. Nehemiah has had time to perfect his quack.

Lion-Hearted

But having a duck's back is nothing if not paired with a lion's heart. One is protective and the other is proactive.

And the lion heart in us looks like this: in spite of difficulty or criticism, stay engaged in the work God has called you to. Don't abandon your post. In your heart pumps the blood of an overcomer. The light is worth the fight, whether that is coming home to fan the flame in the heart of the adopted child who still believes she is an orphan or shining a spotlight on twenty-seven million people who are still enslaved on our earth. Or lighting a candle for the broken-homed fourth-grade students you teach. Or cheering on a girlfriend when she finds her light and stands in it. Aw, friends, now that—that's going to take a lion's heart.

Don't miss it when God calls you to say to hurting hearts, "You're worth this fight. Jesus believes it and so do I."

Ask God to gift you with a heart like the Lion of the tribe of Judah.

Ask God to give you a back like a duck's.

And, if necessary, *ask God to help you do it, despite the critics.*

Sparkler: Have you ever experienced the sting of overly judgmental criticism? If so, how did you weather that experience? Did you have a duck's back and lion's heart, or did you take the criticism in, cherishing it too deeply? How do you feel about the fact that criticism is a part of the journey on this broken terra firma? List several things you will decide *now* that you will do when it comes your way.

16

The Show Must Go On

Nevertheless, I tell you the truth: it is to your advantage that I go away, for if I do not go away, the Helper will not come to you. But if I go, I will send him to you.

John 16:7 ESV

Everybody remembers the moment.

Even if you didn't see it firsthand, you probably remember the moment. By this time, it has been woven into our national collective story. I remember watching it firsthand.

The year was 1996. The Olympics in Atlanta. The Americans were fighting for team gold in women's gymnastics. They were close to snagging the gold medal, but a second well-executed vault by the four-foot-eight Kerri Strug would all but clinch it. The story goes that the gymnast knew she was pretty injured, having heard an inauspicious pop on the previous exercise. But team glory was at stake. So, she turned and asked her coach about trying again. And the coach, the legendary Béla Károlyi, basically said, "Give me one more." Give me one more.

Which she did.

With a shredded ankle, Kerri took off down the runway, running, gaining speed, flying on adrenaline. She performed her vault and stuck the landing; then she dropped to the mat in misery. The iconic picture of the event, fittingly, is of Kerri—wrapped ankle and all—in her coach's arms. She would not be able to compete in her upcoming individual events. But Team America won gold, not in small part due to what Kerri had done that day. She had sacrificed herself for something bigger than herself.[1]

In her broken-bodied and beautiful act, her life said, "The show must go on."

This adage, birthed from the theater, can now be said of most any situation, mundane or momentous, majestic or minute. Think of it this way. "The show," even in theater, equals the story. So the show "going on" can refer to the gymnast who just stuck an impossible landing, or to the new mom who is gritting her way through the first day back on the job. The show—think story—must go on.

The phrase simply means that when we are in the middle of something bigger than we are, something important, and the unforeseen occurs, we must summon the inner fortitude to move through the difficulty and bring the thing, the show, the day, to its best possible conclusion. Against daunting odds, we've got to bring the talk, the gymnastic routine, the graduation, the sermon, the meeting, all the way through.

No matter the slips and stumbles, we're going to take the mountain one step at a time until we summit. We will finish. Because finishing isn't just about us, it is about the people we've been called to. Finishing well is about something and someone bigger.

All of that is at the true heart of the phrase "The show must go on."

I've had two particular times onstage when I was faced with a "show must go on" moment. The first was one where God graciously gave me the inner calm to help the show go on, and the other? Well, in that case I needed a little help from a plucky cheerleader. For kicks and grins, let's call them Exhibit A and Exhibit B.

Exhibit A: Please, Go On

I was standing in an arena, performing one of the more important moments in a new drama I had written. My character, Robin, who struggled with an eating disorder, had finally gathered the bravery to see a Christian counselor after a fifteen-year battle with the mirror. In other words, it was *the* moment of the piece. She makes the long walk to the counselor's chair to begin giving up her heart's deep pain, sits, and opens her mouth to speak, and then . . .

. . . The power went out. All of it. Lights, microphones, A/C. It was as if the sun had blown a fuse. The whole arena lay in darkness. You could hear gasps and then blanketed silence, as everyone waited on what would happen next. My actor instincts came to life and brought words along with them: *the show must go on.*

Whatever it takes, the show must go on.

Even in the abject blackness, I was thinking, *The. Show. Must. Go. On.* But how? How in the world would the show go on if the twenty thousand or so people in the audience couldn't hear or see? Everything inside got super-focused, as I mentally flipped through options.

At that very moment, the emergency generator whirled on, illuminating the arena aisles just enough so the action on stage could be seen in shadowy relief. There were still no stage lights and no microphones, but there was just enough light to be seen and to see by. That would have to be enough. Muscle memory kicked in. I inhaled deeply enough to pop my diaphragm and continued with the scene, gutting out the words. No counseling client has ever divulged her heart more loudly. I nearly screamed the character's truth. There was dead silence in the arena as my voice echoed back to me—slowly, loudly, carefully—on the stage. Without any technical assistance, the mini one-woman drama was going forward. We wouldn't leave Robin hanging with no hope. And we wouldn't leave the women who were counting on Robin's story to inject some hope into their own stories without a fitting conclusion.

The show was going on—and so was the story. Perhaps someone in that audience needed to follow that character's particular arc toward healing. For what seemed to be an eternity, I continued on, near-yelling Robin's intimate confession to the empty chair that represented her Christian counselor, Rose.

And then the sound came: the odd hum of electricity coursing though the system, finally releasing into glorious bursts of lights. It was like God had said, "Let there be light!" And there was. And there was sound too. My voice, amplified by my diaphragm and years of training, finally had assistance. I could be heard without yelling. The camera lights glowed, indicating that they were beaming the image across the arena on the Jumbotron. We had power, folks. That night the lights came back on in the arena.

I took a deep breath, reorienting myself, prepping to bring the drama to a conclusion, when an unusual thing happened—the whole arena burst into extended applause. Right in the middle of the piece. I sat in the counselor's office. Waiting. Pausing. I knew that the applause wasn't for me per se. It was for the moment. It was recognition for an oddly transcendent moment, when we all determined, collectively, that the story was bigger than anything else. It was bigger than an actress or technical difficulty or an arena plunged into utter darkness.

And as far as the kingdom is concerned, the spiritual Story is bigger than any one of us, and the Story goes on. I think very specifically of how God first commissions Joshua, right before he is to take the people of Israel across the Jordan at flood stage. God says, "Now, Moses my servant is dead; now, you and all these people need to consecrate yourselves and cross over the river" (Josh. 1:2, paraphrase). In other words, "My people are appointed to take the Promised Land, and though Moses is gone, Joshua, I need you to step in and take the leadership reins, assuring that the great work of grace continues."

The story—the show—goes on.

In the darkened arena, I experienced that principle vividly. I was possessed of a clearheaded calm and knew what to do when the unexpected happened, but there was another time when not only did I cause the mistake, but I couldn't cover it.

Exhibit B: Showstopper

I was still in New York, in the Eugene O'Neill Theater. I was probably nearing performance number thirty-five or so in one of the principal roles I was tasked with covering for the Broadway run. For this particular performance, I had been given little warning about "going on." That was nothing new. I'd actually "gone on" in the middle of the show several times before.

Once, I was pulled to play the schoolmarm, Miss Lynch, at intermission. The midfifties Tony nominee usually playing that part had suffered an injury, and they needed me to cover. I can remember being roughly pulled from Gertie's ensemble track, as wigs were ripped off and put on, and they made the announcement to the packed-out house, "This evening the role of Miss Lynch will now be played by. . . ." In the audience's eye, the character went from fifties and five feet two to six feet and age twenty-four in an instant. Though not terribly common in the middle of a show, this was not unheard of for New York audiences. The show had to go on, and the show was bigger than one person. So the audience accepted the height and age change, and on the story went.

For the assignment in question, on this particular night I had a little more warning, but not much. I got to the theater thinking I was doing Gertie, and was met with the news that I would be going on as one of the main characters. I felt foggy and a little off my game, like my mind was a molasses swamp. (More on this later.) But, hey! The show had to go on! I'd done this particular role many times over by this point.

In one of the quick-change moments, when I had to change costumes lickety-split, I ran offstage and one of the dressers (folks hired to dress actors) threw on my character's jacket. Back onstage, there I was, ready for the 1950s shenanigans. In the particular scene, I was supposed to throw on some crazy glasses—that were supposed to be preset in the character's jacket pocket. According to the book, I was supposed to throw them on and ask the other gals on stage how they liked my new, funky glasses.

The moment was approaching, as I reached into my pocket. The glasses weren't there. They had not been preset. In my haze I had not double-checked my props, and for some reason the dresser had forgotten them too. Reaching into the empty pocket, I froze. After years in the theater and boatloads of cumulative performances, I froze like an ice sculpture. Someone finally asked me, "Hey, aren't you going to get some glasses?" They were trying to save the moment. And I said, "No." You read that correctly. I said, "No."

Now, friends, saying "no" is breaking one of the cardinal rules of the theater—it's called "blocking the moment," and I had been trained for years at CMU never to do it. Blocking is an improv term—and, in an oversimplified nutshell, it means doing anything that blocks the continuance of the scene. Hear this with spiritual ears; saying "No" in this particular context stops the story. Had I not been blocking, I would have just replied, "Yes, and when I do get them, they are gonna be uh-mazing!" That would have broadcast to the other actors that the sunglasses were missing and to carry on. But when I said "No," the show ground to a halt. What were they supposed to say? Even with trained comedians and Broadway vets, awkward silence filled the stage for maybe forty seconds as everyone tried to recover. We all flubbed and floundered, terribly, until another actress, playing a plucky cheerleader, finally entered the stage, moving the show forward a few pages. It was a crazy, clumsy, uncomfortable, hot mess.

But the show still went on.

Whether the showstopping moment goes something like the arena event, where God gave me a supernatural sense of calm, or it goes like it did that one Broadway night when my internal fuses blew, I want you to know that, as it has been said, failure isn't fatal. Whether the source is failed lights or a failed brain, *the Story is still king. And even mistakes cannot stop it.*

The next day, I would show up at the theater and report for work. I would play the role I made the mistake in many more times before I ultimately left the show to move home to Greensboro. Even the artistic staff knew that one mistake didn't disqualify me—my one failure didn't trump the other 649 (or so) performances.

I wish I could press that into your heart. *Failure cannot define you.* Not if you don't allow it to do so. God is bigger than every failure you have ever experienced or caused. In fact, God seems to take special delight in dusting off people who have failed and making the spiritual Story go on through them.

Peter's rashness didn't stop him from becoming the rock. Joseph's teenaged swagger didn't stop him from becoming Pharaoh's second-in-command. Moses's crime of murder didn't stop him from becoming Yahweh's mouthpiece. David's affair didn't stop him from becoming the man after God's own heart. You've heard it said—failure isn't fatal. It simply isn't.

Especially not in Jesus's hands. *In fact, the safest place for our failure is in the hands of Jesus.*

Cast your care, cast your failure, cast your fault on Jesus, and then stand back up. Take a step toward him. And shine.

Sparkler: Have you stopped your own show? Friend, if you have stepped out of the Story, would you consider rejoining us there? We need you. Did you once inhabit your place with humility and grace, and something came—perhaps an unexpected jolt—where the physical lights went out on you, or an internal kink, like when my brain ground to a halt? Would you consider rejoining us?

17

Blackouts and Glow Tape

The Word gave life to everything that was
created,
and his life brought light to everyone.
The light shines in the darkness,
and the darkness can never extinguish it.

John 1:4–5 NLT

I've always loved the stars, but not the darkness in which
they exist.

Years ago, an event took place in Pelion, South Carolina, that featured both in equal roles. One Thanksgiving
vacation—late at night—I went outside my aunt's South
Carolina home to take a walk. The stars looked so perfect
that I decided to lie on the ground. Strange, perhaps, but hey,
for years I gardened at midnight. There's no accounting for
odd, and life is still beautiful in the dark.

It was a black night. To my eyes, the stars shone differently there. No headlights or streetlights to compete with their glory. I lay flat on the supporting sand, awed at the constant constellations. Earth's night-lights writ large. Some report feeling small and inconsequential when stargazing. I always feel both small *and* deeply consequential to the God of the universe under their twinkle—connected to a story that will endure far longer than the quick flame of my life. Like ancient seafarers who navigated the oceans by the constellations, I have often navigated my life by those same stars.

I don't know how long I star-bathed under the Carolina sky.

I felt the muzzle first on my forehead, then heard the sniff, then saw the huge black shadow cover my eyes. The stars went out as the dog sniffed down my face. Everything got still as I instantly used my sweetest voice to let the big thing know I was no threat. I didn't move. I prayed in my head.

Things get real clear in the dark.

Within seconds I sensed the intimidating and very large dog wasn't going to attack me, and so I sat up, careful to keep my back to it, in case it changed its mind. Slowly I stood, all the while keeping my voice high and light—"goooood boy"— and turned to make a determined beeline toward my aunt's house. It seemed to want to follow me. I don't know if it did, because I didn't look back. I walked toward the light of her house, burning in the dark, opened the door, and went inside.

Blackout

Even as a young child, I can remember my almost pathological need for light during the night. I double-checked with my mom or dad about leaving the door open just so. Just another inch. I was a midnight waker and remember being scared and disoriented if I couldn't see any light, especially if I had to go into my parents' bedroom or navigate to the restroom. That light led the way.

The theater has its own kind of night-light for special use when the lights go dark or particularly when what is called a "blackout" happens. A "blackout" is that theatrical moment when the lights go out like a flipped switch. They don't dim or fade slowly. Often "blackouts" are used at the end of an act or after a big musical moment. What keeps the actor from stepping off the lip of the stage or from careening into a column in the wings is something called glow tape. Every peril in the dark will have been marked with a small piece of tape that glows in the dark. The special tape charges when the lights are on, so that it glows when the lights go out. It doesn't shine brightly enough to be noticeable to the audience, but because the actor is close enough to the slight glow, the actor can see it, and follow its "just enough" glow to take the next safe step.

Dark Night of the Soul

Almost two decades after the onstage disaster of the missing sunglasses, I would come to understand that the odd haze I felt that particular night, and probably my inability to respond to the missing prop as I'd been trained, was due to undiagnosed depression. The big black dog of depression, as Winston Churchill aptly named it, had followed me home to my Manhattan apartment and had probably been stalking me for large portions of my life.

But I didn't know that in New York. Not then. I was just "exhausted." Sleeping three or four hours at night intermittently for almost two years, accompanied by no appetite, was simply "stress." "Stress" and maybe "heartbreak" too, I thought. Even though I was living the dream, a tough young-love breakup sent me reeling and kept me wide awake. During this period my precious first cousin, Ashleigh, died by suicide. A true beauty, inside and out, her list of creative and academic accomplishments reads like that of a woman three times her age. She was a rare gift and she needed more time, but that is exactly what suicide denies you—time. She had recently turned twenty. I can only imagine the innumerable gifts she would have brought this earth had she only stayed.

Though my lows never reached my sweet family member's depths, I knew what it was to despair, to beg God for sleep. To claw for some short escape from the pain. To make deals with my body—just one more bite—one more step. To do unwise things—like walking around Manhattan at 4 a.m.— simply because I couldn't stand one more night sleepless.

Remember, friends, this was the midnineties, and there wasn't a deep understanding of getting medical help immediately for depression. I didn't even know it was depression. That word wasn't uttered much then. And as is still the case in some circles, there was a stigma to admitting to any such struggle—in the church or elsewhere. I am glad that is changing and applaud those who bravely share their stories of struggle and strength. It wasn't until nearly fifteen years after New York that I grasped a truer understanding of my own fight.

Back then all I knew was that I was winding through a dark maze and desperately needed God to give me some spiritual glow tape for what was a long night walk. And it happened in the simplest of ways.

I attended a church service that happened to meet in a converted theater. (Irony of ironies!) The place looked like the United Nations. Every tribe and kindred was represented, and every tongue was raised in worship. Amazed, I sat in the balcony, lifted and buoyed. I had found a lighthouse that I could run into week after week. Near the end of the service, I did something I have never done before or since. I wrote on a torn-off corner of the bulletin something as bald as, "Hey. I'm sort of new here in the city. Don't really have a ton of Christian friends. Wanna get coffee sometime?" I turned around to the gaggle of girls behind me and handed it to the raven-haired girl, mostly because she looked willing to receive my note. She read it and passed back her own note. "Yes!" it said. After the service, because of a passed note, we made a coffee date.

Several days later we sat, talking life and loss and Jesus. Her name was Lisa. Lisa's life had included starring on Broadway, film, and a current (at the time) long run as a soap star. I had no idea at the time of the passed note that we had a performer's life in common; I just knew she shone with the light of Jesus in a way that drew me in.

We got each other. She didn't care if we hung out late at night. We prayed for each other. We cheered each other on as we each found the love of our lives. Interestingly, both of us wound up in ministry and remain so to this day—both using our gifts but in different ways. We still cheer each other on, though two decades have passed since the times we held up each other's arms during midnight in Manhattan. Her friendship, found in the body of Jesus, was my New York glow tape.

What am I getting at with this story? A couple of things, I suppose. One: please don't equate shining for Christ with a life devoid of difficulty. I think that belief is one big spiritual myth! That we can only really shine when we are without struggle? That God is reluctant to somehow use broken women and men to ignite a broken world? Nonsense! When we finally experience the eternal hello of heaven, I believe countless saints' lives and stories will stand in stark contrast to this potent light killer.

Second, we must remember that we are not responsible for the light; we are only responsible to show up to it when it comes, even when messy and spun. Jesus is the Light. We are the Light-bearers.

I learned that firsthand in New York. Even though I experienced significant emotional pain, I also experienced more spiritual growth than I ever had to that point. I learned to hurt with hope and to wait with wonder. I was more blessed in the giving than the getting. After years of being suspicious about friendship, it was friendship that God used to dot the night sky with stars.

And perhaps most precious to me: I learned that God will use anyone—even a sometimes brokenhearted actress who hung on to the truth that God would turn her darkness into light.

Eternal Flame

It will happen tonight in theaters the world over. I wish you could see it.

The show is done. The audience, actors, and crew have left the building. A person has moved onto the darkened stage and set the object down. It will be plugged in, the knob turned. The shadeless bulb will shine like a beacon.

Tonight, like every other night, the ghost lights of the theater will burn.

The source of the tradition is disputed. Some say the night-time ignition of the "ghost light" began as a way to keep ghosts from wreaking havoc on productions. The thought was, the "ghosts" could have their own performance at night by the light of the ghost light and would therefore leave the actual play alone. Some say the ghost light was born of pure safety. If someone had to enter the theater in the dead of night for some reason, there had to be a way to safely navigate. No one can truly say where the tradition stems from, but it is a tradition that continues to this very day—or night, rather—in almost every live-performance theater you have ever attended.

For me, the beauty of the tradition is found in its symbolism and name—"ghost light." As believers we have a ghost light, too, found in the illuminating power of the Holy Spirit, who is often called the Holy Ghost, and is symbolized by a flame.

Recently I emailed a friend, who happens to be the head of a historical theater, to ask about ghost lights in his theater. "Do you still use a ghost light?" I asked. I wondered if this nightly tradition might have lost its luster. He immediately wrote back that they did indeed. Every night for thirty-one years. For over 10,000 nights that ghost light has burned faithfully. It's never once left the house dark, without a flame through the watches of the night.

Friend, in the darkest season you will ever wrestle through—be it disappointment or depression or disaster or death—your God promises to leave a light burning for you, giving you enough light for the next step. Love, as the anonymous quote says, is the only game in town not called on account of the dark. Light has shined in the darkness, and the darkness has not overcome it (John 1:5).

Your ghost light flames eternal. Take that with you into the dark.

Sparkler: If you feel you are in the middle of a dark night, how my heart goes out to you. It can be so difficult to weather, but Jesus is faithful to you in that tender place. I pray if you find yourself in a dark night of the soul, that the Lord will impress into your heart where your light is in a tangible way—like he did for me in the body of Christ, daring me to step back into friendship. No matter where you are, there is a light on for you, friend.

18

The Role of a Lifetime

Now on the first day of the week Mary Magdalene came to the tomb early, while it was still dark.

John 20:1 ESV

*M*any actors are in a passionate hunt for the role of a lifetime.

That magical fit happens after a long, winding journey, marked with great triumphs and, often, equally great trip-ups. But for those who stay engaged in the journey, the day comes when the actor and the role strike like a flame and wood. Something ignites. The actor feels: *This is it! This is the role I was made for. The role I was born to play! Everything from here on out will be different because of this one role.*

I admit, the role of a lifetime somewhat eluded me as an actor. I can point to many pivotal roles in my tenure as a live performer—ones that catapulted me artistically or opened opportunity's doors, but not *the one* where I could doubtlessly declare, "Now, that one right there, that was the golden ticket." I never found the role of a lifetime in the lights of the world.

But I did find it in the Light of the World.

My lifetime role came to me when I was ushered into the kingdom. It came when I encountered the Director of the ages, Jesus. The One who helped me drop the brave act. The One who walked me all the way to the light pooling on his God-stage. The One who helped me leave the shadows, saying, "See that light, kid? In me, that's yours. Go find it and stand there—weakness and wonder alike—until I say it's time to move on. And then we'll go find another light, you and me."

For me, chasing Christ has been *the* role of a lifetime. That role entails being seen—when, how, and where God directs—so that God himself can be easier to see. In different seasons, the light looks different, and the size of the audience matters not a whit, but the call to shine has never lost its luster for me.

What a relief when I finally stepped into the role of a lifetime. When I finally knew.

Standing before an audience of thousands, I wonder if David knew it.

Standing before an audience of few, I wonder if Queen Esther knew it.

Standing before an audience of One, I wonder if Mary of Magdala knew it.

Shine: *Mary of Magdala's Moment*

I will make an attempt to make an account of these things.

Unnatural darkness covered us. The Drama of the Ages unfolded in shadowy, starless relief.

After Jesus had spoken his final earthly benediction, banishing his spirit from his body, he exhaled one more time. The Breath of Life drained of breath. Just as he predicted. Absorbing all sin into his marrow until he was consumed with it. Became it.

The dark hour pulsed with the war-drum thud of men beating their chests as they exited the scene. Through the confusing night, we women remained—we were not hunted like the men, and so we could stay close. Following him like small shadows, we trailed Joseph of Arimathea and Nicodemus as they requested his destroyed body, wrapped it in the finest linen, and laid it in a virgin garden tomb. Though dead, no death should taint him. We counted our steps in the dark to the place he had been laid. We navigated by the stars.

And then we went home to prepare the spices that would preserve the body of God-in-Flesh. Our tears fell in the mixture. In accordance with the command of the Book, we rested on the Sabbath, though my own body did not sleep in the great waiting. I wrestled with the words he had spoken to us previously, promising us that death would not speak last. But I had seen the death with my own eyes, and wondered who could trounce a death like the brutal death of the cross.

It was dark yet again when we rose after the longest Sabbath I had ever known. My eyes had grown accustomed to the dimness. We set out to the rock-hewn tomb to dress his body, the last act of love we could give the One who so loved the world. We walked in quiet, our footfalls and breathing the only sound in the night. As we reached the place, we expected to see the stone still in place; we expected to perhaps beg the soldiers to move it for us that we might attend him. If they killed us for asking, I, for one, was ready for their sword.

But in the breaking dawn, we saw the monolith had already been rolled away. We ran; the three of us ran through the mouth of the tomb, expecting to see the linen-wrapped body of the Great One. But all that remained was an empty slab, crisscrossed with strips of linen unwound. I instantly remembered Lazarus back from the dead.

Our bodies gave way under the weight; we three fell to the earth and bowed, the spices and nard spilling and breaking open as we did, filling the tomb with scent. Terror and wonder tangled. Had someone moved him? Had he moved himself? Later I would realize I was sobbing.

Through tears, I saw the lower half of two figures standing by. I knew they were not soldiers come to kill us. Nor two of the Eleven come to join us. These were not men of any sort. These were angelic clarions, glowing with the brilliance of a sustained lightning strike. I shielded my eyes as I lifted my head, straining like a child to see in another world's shine.

"Why do you look for the living among the dead? He is not here. He is risen! Remember how he told you when he was still with you in Galilee. The Son of Man must be delivered into the hands of sinful men, be crucified and on the third day be raised again." It all flooded back to me. Resurrection: the great "again" of God. He would come again. Rise again. Live again.

Again.

We ran, hitching our skirts as high as we could, to run without tripping. We galloped—all of us. We ran like the language of the Psalms: "The Lord announces the word, and the women who proclaim it are a mighty throng." We ran like a holy herd with the Word, our lungs and legs straining against the pace we had set for ourselves.

Finally, we reached the Eleven. We stumbled in: sweat-drenched, winded. They stood—sleepless, red-eyed, bereft. The news spilled like a babble from us. I began recounting the details. Of the dark night giving way to dawn and the stone rolled away. Of angels and strange words.

And then we waited for their reply.

All that answered us was silence. The silence of disbelief.

One of them—to this day I do not know who—grunted, "Nonsense." Only Peter, Peter, more gaunt and cried-out than any of them, moved. He approached me and stared into my face, as if to say, "Mary of Magdala, do you tell the truth?" I nodded my head once. At this, he turned and ran from the room. John followed on his heels. Never one far behind the other.

I followed them back to the tomb, standing outside, to see what they would make of the evidence. I wept and waited. Oddly, I noticed my own sandaled feet—feet that had carried me to bereft and beautiful places. Torn and dirty, but useful still. Still my own. Peter exited the tomb, looking as spun as a storm-tossed sailor. John followed. Worried looks flitted across their faces as daylight grew. They could not be seen at an empty tomb, lest they be accused by our occupiers of graverobbing. They returned to the others. I remained.

I stood, spent. Perhaps all of it was a hysteria. If the Eleven had not believed, why should I? If Peter and John did not exit the tomb with shouts of victory, perhaps defeat had won the day. Perhaps he had not risen but had only been removed. Removed from us, for all time.

There in the garden, I wept tears, ancient and new. I wept for all the days I had lived Christ-less. I wept for the wonder he brought to my wounds and for what living without his voice in the world meant for the world. And for me.

I wept for the better part of the morning. When I could stand no more, I crawled to the tomb and peered in, to be close to the last place he had been. I thought I hallucinated again—as the angels were there, sitting this time, saying, "Woman, why are you crying?" Caught between the angelic evidence and the doubt of those closest to him, I said, "They have taken my Lord away, and I do not know where they have put him."

At this, I felt another standing behind me. I turned, not recognizing the form, but recognizing the melody of the voice, as it asked the same angelic question, "Woman, why are you crying? Who is it you are looking for?"

I cry because the Light of the World has been snuffed out. I look for the Bright Morning Star, but he has been consumed by darkness. I thought it, but did not say it.

I believed the man speaking was a gardener, perhaps sent by Joseph of Arimathea to tend the beauty of the place that held so much pain for those of us who loved him. And then the odd gardener said one word. One word that happened to be my name. *Mary.* The Voice that commanded, "Let there be Light!" said my name. In that moment, there could be no mistaking.

My Light. My Life.

"Teacher," is what I said in response, rushing and clinging to him, as if he were the only candle in a world gone black.

"Do not hold on to Me, for I have not yet returned to my Father. Go instead to my brothers, and tell them, 'I am returning to my Father and your Father, to My God and your God.'"

A million reasons came why he should choose another. But in the end, I simply said yes.

I ran, forever ruined for ordinary things.

I ran with the news that would split the ages.

I fled the shadows and ran into the full light of day.[1]

The Role of a Lifetime

In that moment, standing outside the twice-visited tomb, Jesus invites Mary Magdalene to join him in the role of a lifetime. This is Mary's "go into the world and preach the Good News" moment. This is her life's defining moment. This is her shout-out to shine, so that the Light of the World might flame eternal in the hearts of men and women the creation over. And she accepts the charge.

Mary accepts Jesus's call to shine as herself. Just regular old Mary. No brave act. No character shoes. No show. Just the showing up. She doesn't come as a lofty mouthpiece, dignified and honored to carry such news. No, she comes weak and wild in her grief. Spun and spent. Bereft and broken when she finally hears her own, true name in his mouth. "Mary." And then when she hears her name, she knows Who this is that is calling her to come out of the shadows for his sake, for our sake.

She steps into her eternal light and stands bravely, because Jesus said, "This moment matters. They need to know eternity's door is flung wide open for all who believe, and I want you, Mary, to tell them." Talk about a God-stage. Talk about playing the role of a lifetime in the capital *D* Drama.

Curtain Closer

So many people procrastinate over beginnings. I procrastinate over endings.

I'm all in for the launch of a new adventure, but when it's time to take a final bow and exit the building, I'm all out, emotionally speaking. I know the Scripture says, "Finishing is better than starting" (Eccles. 7:8 NLT), but I struggle to get my emotional ducks to line up in a row.

This morning I planted my patootie in my old leather writing chair—and pondered all this ending ambivalence, wondering why I felt so conflicted. At first I thought it was all the common reasons a writer might feel this way: *Have I been clear enough? Made Jesus the easiest person on the page to see? Maybe just one more chapter. . . .* In the end, I realize those things will be for you to weigh. But as I sat with those questions, underneath it all, I realized my struggle with the ending reflected a very real truth about everything we have discussed so far: I don't like endings, because the truth is, the journey never really ends.

This journey of following Jesus into the light he provides— of taking off the character shoes. Of shining, despite the critics. Of joining him in the capital *D* Drama. Of stepping into the role of a lifetime. This journey doesn't end. It never ceases. In Philippians 1, Paul trumpets this truth when he says this (vv. 6–7, paraphrase):

Being confident of this: He Who began a good work in you will bring it all the way to completion until the day of Christ Jesus. It is right to feel this way about you, since I have you all in my heart.

That does my soul good. Until the day of Christ Jesus—this capital *D* Drama won't have its curtain closed until the day of Jesus. The Great Story goes on. And the One who is carrying it on is Jesus himself. What relief. What hope. What joy.

Our Turn

Along the way, we will stumble many times.

But being confident in his grace, there will be many more times that we stand.

There will be those grace-saturated moments when we finally exit the shadows and dare to follow our trustworthy Director all the way to the light he provides. Times we spit out the poisonous character names. Times when we fling off the character shoes and dare to take the stage with him, even in our weakness. Times when we wait patiently in the wings and understudy people worth studying. Times when we thank God that it's not our turn. Times when we abandon wanting someone else's story, knowing that nobody else's story is as exciting as the one Jesus is inviting us to. Times when we move with grace to a new place. Times when we step into the role of a lifetime.

Eternal Flame

The call remains. And in the few blink-eyed moments we have on this earth, if we keep our hearts open and pliable to our great Director, I believe with all my heart that we will hear him whisper:

> *It's time to leave the shadows, child.*
> *See that light pooling out there?*
> *Let's step into it, you and me.*
> *It's time to shine.*

> *Arise, shine, for your light has come.*

Acknowledgments

I can no other answer make but thanks,
And thanks, and ever thanks.
                              Twelfth Night, Act II, scene 3

Jonathan: You are the greatest proof of God's existence this gal will ever receive on this side of eternity. The best is ahead.

Luke and Levi: When you see the moon and sun (and even when you can't), my love for you is ever-present. Thank you for the delightful gift of being your mom.

Mom: This book is a daughter's answer to your brave statement that day. We miss you more than we can possibly say. Until the temporary good-bye gives way to the eternal hello.

Jim (My Brotha!), Dad, Jan, Jetta, and Jim, Carolyn, Sherrie and Bill, Sandy and Rick, as well as the extended Metcalf, Allen, and Crout/Dunbar families: Your goodness is the great foundation and wellspring of my life.

Pastor Steve and Sarah Berger: For two decades of dear friendship, guidance, and unadulterated God-focus, thank you.

Grace Chapel staff, family, and arts ministries: You beautiful living organism, you. Humbled to be numbered among your throng.

Lisa Jackson, agent extraordinaire: Your calm voice, your well-timed encouragement, your "you-ness" make me eternally glad (and honored) to be in your nest at Alive.

Vicki Crumpton: Your laser-like insight, your steady hand, your surgical precision have been God's incredible mercies to this first-time author. I am lucky to call you editor and friend.

Wendy Wetzel, Erin Smith, Laura Peterson, Kristin Kornoelje, and the entire Revell team: Thank you for inviting me to dance. I can't wait to see where God's choreography takes us.

The #8 (Heather, Heather, Tammy, Charlie, Brian, Kev): There are no words. Just ever-thanks.

Lisa Harper: For belief that buoyed. For wisdom that guided. For generosity that astounded.

Darlene Grieme and Stone Island: No one else on this planet runs as flat-out as you for the kingdom. So grateful.

Dan Seaman, Terry and Robin Sartain, Arthur Giron, Livestock Players (Barabra), CMU professors, directors, and classmates, Razz-Ma-Tazz (Carole), Clay Gillespie: Thank you for being among the innumerable good directors in my life.

Patsy Clairmont, Mary Graham, Nicole Johnson, Marilyn Meberg, Sandi Patty, Anita Renfroe, Mandisa, Nicole C. Mullen, Luci Swindoll, Sheila Walsh, Lisa Whelchel: Three years in the WOF sphere were a master class in all things. Thank you for allowing me to study under you.

Lori McGinnis, Evelyn Leonard, Teasi and Bill Cannon, Jake and Amy Spencer, Michele and Matt Reddick, Kandi and George McIntyre, Linda Dion, Lisa Southard, Lisa and Brad Guice, the Eatons, the Childs, the Camps, Loral Peppon, Penny Hunter, Olivia Heard, Joanie Stewart, Penny Blum, Shawn King, Suzanne Metcalf, Emily Winslow Stark, Ginna Claire Mason, Dawn and JT Taylor, Christy Haines, the Hamiltons, the Rhodes, the Ekes, the Cellas and Brimstead Neighbors: For loving through the many seasons that life on this terra firma brings.

Amy and David Lowry: For many faithful and loving years.

For all the women's ministry directors who have become sisters-in-arms: Your work to bring Jesus to the women you are tasked with serving is seen.

Special thanks to my friend R. D. Meyers for his fantastic work on the harmony of the Gospels in his book, *The Ministry of Jesus*. I'm indebted to him for the order of events of the resurrection account.

The Bright and Morning Star: You have relentlessly turned my darkness into everlasting light. I am lost without you.

A portion of all author's proceeds will go to support the work of the International Justice Mission. For more information about their work, go to www.IJM.org

Notes

Chapter 1 All the World's a Stage

1. "I Just Showed Up to My Own Life." Music and Lyrics By: Sara Groves & Joel Hanson © 2005 Sara Groves Music (ASCAP) (admin. By Music Services)/Where's Rocky Music Publishing (BMI) All Rights Reserved. Used by Permission.

2. *Merriam-Webster Collegiate Dictionary Online*, s.v. "drama," accessed February 8, 2017, http://unabridged.merriam-webster.com/collegiate/drama.

3. Henry Miller, *The Books in My Life* (New Directions Publishing, 1969), 167.

4. Holly Corbett, "Understanding Male Vulnerability," *Redbook*, September 12, 2012, http://www.redbookmag.com/love-sex/mens-perspective/interviews/a14409/brene-brown-shame-vulnerability/.

Chapter 2 The Brave Act and Character Shoes

1. C. S. Lewis, *The Screwtape Letters* (West Chicago: Lord and King, 1976), 48, emphasis mine.

2. Kristen Weir, "The Pain of Social Rejection," *Monitor on Psychology* 43, no. 4 (April 2012), www.apa.org/monitor/2012/04/rejection.aspx.

3. Hans Christian Andersen, *Hans Christian Andersen's Complete Fairy Tales*, trans. Jean P. Hersholt (San Diego: Canterbury Classics, 2014).

4. I am thankful to Brene Brown's quote for enlightening me about the difference between belonging and fitting in. www.good reads.com/quotes/6854431.

Chapter 3 Ancient Character Shoes

1. For further information, see H. D. M. Spence and Joseph S. Exell, eds., *The Pulpit Commentary*, vol. 4 (Grand Rapids: Eerdmans, 1978), 324–330.

2. Ibid., 329.

Chapter 4 What's in a Name?

1. William Shakespeare, *Romeo and Juliet*, act 2, scene 2, Shakespeare-Online.com, http://www.shakespeare-online.com/plays/balconyscene/romeoandjulietbalconyscene.html, emphasis mine.

2. Thanks to John and Stasi Eldredge for their reflections on the act of naming in "August Newsletter," Ransomed Heart, August 2012, https://www.ransomedheart.com/sites/default/files/u117861/2012_august_newsletter.pdf.

3. I'm grateful to Stasi Eldredge for this insight on the way God says our names. See "He Calls You by Name," Ransomed Heart, April 2, 2013, https://www.ransomedheart.com/blogs/stasi/he-calls-you-name.

4. Ibid.

5. T. Desmond Alexander, "Genesis," in *ESV Study Bible*, ed. Lane T. Dennis et al. (Wheaton, IL: Crossway, 2008), 108.

Chapter 5 Spitting Out the Poison

1. "Tragic Flaw," LiteraryDevices.net, accessed March 31, 2017, https://literarydevices.net/tragic-flaw/.

Chapter 7 Empty Spotlights

1. Frederick Buechner, *Secrets in the Dark: A Life in Sermons* (New York: HarperCollins, 2006), 39.

Chapter 8 Finer Points of Light

1. Lisa Harper, personal correspondence.

Chapter 9 Trusting the Director

1. Seale Ballenger, *Hell's Belles: A Tribute to the Spitfires, Bad Seeds & Steel Magnolias of the New and Old South* (Berkeley, CA: Conari Press, 1997), 71.

2. See Luke 8:29; John 4:7b; Mark 4:40; Matthew 9:28 ESV; Matthew 20:22 ESV; John 21:17; John 6:67 ESV; John 5:6 ESV; John 20:15.

Chapter 10 You Are What You Rehearse

1. *Online Etymology Dictionary*, s.v. "rehearsal," accessed February 13, 2017, http://www.etymonline.com/index.php?term =rehearse.

Chapter 11 Waiting in the Wings

1. Charles H. Spurgeon, "The Treasury of David: Psalm 130, Verse 5," The Spurgeon Archive, accessed February 13, 2017, http://www.spurgeon.org/treasury/ps130.php.

2. *Brown-Driver-Briggs Hebrew and English Lexicon, Unabridged Electronic Database*, s.v. "qavah," accessed February 13, 2017, http://biblehub.com/hebrew/6960.htm.

Chapter 12 Being in the Moment vs. Stealing the Light

1. From *Chess*, 1996, music by Benny Anderson and Björn Ulvaeus, lyrics by Tim Rice.

2. Jonathan Allen, © 2000. All rights reserved.

3. John Piper, "What is That to You? You Follow Me!" Desiring God, October 6, 2006, http://www.desiringgod.org/articles/what -is-that-to-you-you-follow-me.

4. S. Austin Allibone, *Prose Quotations from Socrates to Macaulay* (Philadelphia: J. B. Lippincott & Co., 1880), quoted on

Bartleby.com, accessed February 14, 2017, http://www.bartleby
.com/349/4.html.

Chapter 13 Understudy Graces

1. Robert Jamieson, Andrew Robert Fausset, and David Brown, "Esther 9:26," in *Commentary Critical and Expository on the Whole Bible*, accessed March 30, 2017, http://biblehub.com/commentaries /esther/9-26.htm.

Chapter 15 Despite the Critics

1. "Word Study: Judge and Judgment," In Search of Truth, accessed February 15, 2017, http://www.insearchoftruth.org /articles/word_study_judge.html. See also *Brown-Driver-Briggs Hebrew and English Lexicon, Unabridged Electronic Database*, s.v. "diakrinō," accessed February 15, 2017, http://biblehub.com /greek/1252.htm.

2. Brennan Manning, *The Ragamuffin Gospel: Good News for the Bedraggled, Beat-Up and Burnt Out* (Colorado Springs: Multnomah, 2005), 25.

3. H. D. M. Spence and Joseph S. Exell, eds., *The Pulpit Commentary*, vol. 7 (Grand Rapids: Eerdmans, 1978), 61–62.

4. Ibid.

Chapter 16 The Show Must Go On

1. Filip Bondy, "Kerri Strug Stands Tall on Injured Ankle, Leads US Gymnastics to Team Gold at 1996 Atlanta Olympics," *New York Daily News*, July 24, 1996, http://www.nydailynews.com/sports/more -sports/kerri-stands-tall-sprained-ankle-article-1.2015138.

Chapter 18 The Role of a Lifetime

1. This text is my interpretation of the way Mary might have felt and acted during this encounter with the risen Jesus.

Allison Allen is a graduate of the prestigious Carnegie Mellon University and appeared in approximately 650 performances of the Broadway production of *Grease*. A former Women of Faith dramatist and current Bible teacher, she speaks to women at conferences and retreats around the country, exploring themes of purpose, value, and identity in original and unexpected ways. She lives with her family in Tennessee.

Allison Allen

Let's Keep the Conversation Going...

 / AllisonAllen   @ AllisonAllen    / AllisonAllenSpeaks

AllisonAllen.net